How to nurture and enhance children's
emotional development

Anna-Michele Hantler

Acknowledgements

Firstly, I should like to acknowledge the influence of the following three women:

Margot Sunderland for supporting my creative and playful approach to work with children, and for her desire to get emotional education right for children.

The late Noreen Wetton for nurturing my passion for children's picture books and for sharing her insights into and appreciation of how children make sense of the world.

Jenny Mosley for her unstinting encouragement and her faith in my ability to get my ideas down on paper.

Secondly, I should like to thank all the children I have worked with, who persevered in their difficulties and trusted in my attempts to support them through such times.

Thirdly, I should like to record my thanks to the parents, families and colleagues I have come in contact with, who shared with me their expertise, patience, compassion and struggles. This includes those students from the initial emotional literacy courses held at the Centre for Child Mental Health, and the staff from schools in Stockton-on-Tees, who piloted the massage in schools project with me.

Fourthly, I want to acknowledge the support of Emma Gunn, Jill Wood and Julie Heap, who piloted some of the Draw and Write materials used in this book.

I should, of course, like to thank my family and friends for putting up with my not-so-calm emotional self, and for my lack of attention as I wrote this book.

Finally, I want to thank Corin Redsell and his colleagues at LDA for approaching me to write this book, for their confidence in my ability to produce something of use for classroom practitioners, and for their desire to publish a resource to help make emotions matter.

Dedication

To Simon, my brother, for his words of encouragement.

Permission to photocopy

This book contains materials which may be reproduced by photocopier or other means for use by the purchaser. The permission is granted on the understanding that these copies will be used within the educational establishment of the purchaser. The book and all its contents remain copyright. Copies may be made without reference to the publisher or the licensing scheme for the making of photocopies operated by the Publishers' Licensing Agency.

The right of Anna-Michele Hantler to be identified as the author of this work has been asserted by her in accordance with sections 77 and 78 of the Copyright, Designs and Patents Act 1988.

How to nurture and enhance children's emotional development
MT10771
ISBN-13: 978 1 85503 433 4

© Anna-Michele Hantler
Illustrations © Garry Davies
All rights reserved
First published 2008

Printed in the UK for LDA
Abbeygate House, East Road, Cambridge, CB1 1DB, UK

Contents

Contents

Foreword

This book will be a real asset to anyone following the government's Social and Emotional Aspects of Learning curriculum (SEAL) and the Every Child Matters agenda. It is brimming with practical tools and techniques underpinned by an in-depth knowledge of how children struggle to manage their painful feelings. Anna-Michele has covered all aspects of a child's emotionality: what is happening in the brain and body; the child's perception of self, others and their world as differentiated from that of an adult; their mode and language of expression. The material is presented using a truly delightful writing style that makes you feel as if the author is in the room having a conversation with you. Hence, it is a gripping read, which will engage your emotions and imagination, as well as your thinking.

The book will be a great resource for any teacher or other professional involved in the emotional well-being of children. There are sections on classroom techniques, how to address specific emotions and particular issues, and how to look after your emotional well-being so you can look after that of others. The worksheets bring all the information into the practical realm. Anna-Michele's in-depth knowledge of Draw and Write from her decades of engaging children with this excellent tool will inspire and support you as you use this resource in the classroom.

Dr Margot Sunderland, Director of Education and Training at The Centre for Child Mental Health, London

Introduction

The introduction in primary and secondary schools of Social and Emotional Aspects of Learning (SEAL) brings a curriculum of emotional education for children and young people to the fore. This book sits alongside SEAL, uniting theory and practice. Aimed at the primary practitioner, it encompasses ideas and strategies for addressing the language of everyday feelings, and for supporting children through emotionally difficult times.

Some children will not engage with their external world until they are helped through their internal world.

Some children will not engage with their external world until they are helped through their internal world. In schools we are increasingly in need of a well-equipped tool kit to help them. I should like to share with you in particular the expertise of three influential and inspirational women.

While doing my integrative arts psychotherapy training with Margot Sunderland at the London Institute of Arts and Therapy in Education, I encountered a wealth of creative, inventive and meaningful approaches to emotional exploration.

As a PSHE adviser, I was inspired by the late Noreen Wetton. The Draw and Write technique originated with her. I have adapted it to research all manner of sensitive issues.

Along the way, I met Jenny Mosley and was introduced to her highly practical Quality Circle Time model (QCT) with its whole-school approach to behaviour. Listening systems are a technique of hers that I have used in many settings.

I use all these approaches to deliver and evaluate emotional education through the arts. I encourage you to take time, and to tweak activities and suggestions to suit your children and cultural setting.

Whenever delivering activities designed to explore emotions, ensure that you have appropriate time and support. Remember that worksheets are never intended to stand alone and should be used as a stimulus for discussion and skill development, as an evaluation tool, as a school–home link, to consider ways to change behaviour, to realise that others have similar feelings, and to think through emotional scenarios.

Chapter 1
Why help children with feelings?

If we are to reach real peace in this world ... we shall have to begin with the children.

Mohandas Gandhi

UK statistics
40,000 children on anti-depressants, 50% of children experience bullying, 17,000 excluded annually from school.

We have gone too far in emphasising the value and importance of the purely rational – what IQ measures. Intelligence can come to nothing when emotions hold sway.

Daniel Goleman

As a society we cannot ignore the increasing evidence of poorly managed emotional lives: the disintegration of family life and breakdown of supportive networks, the stress related to overworking or unemployment, the sadness of suffering and abuse in many relationships, the commonality of human misery, anxiety and despair.

Parents spend less time with children than ever before because of insecure, high-pressured workplaces, economic necessity and our increasing materialism. Many children spend more time in front of the television set than in conversation with their parents.

The good news is we now have an impetus towards a more emotionally literate generation of parents and educators. Children need help to sort out the complexities of human relationships. No matter how riveting your teaching or charismatic your approach, some children are at risk of remaining unengaged and emotionally abandoned. The greatest danger of all is that they will give up on themselves.

IQ versus EQ?

Schools remain under pressure to perform academically and staff are exhausted by ever more initiatives and constant changes. May we conclude that the push for the best results has come at a cost? Research suggests that 70–80 per cent of our success is shaped by our emotional quotient (EQ) – our ability to manage our emotional lives effectively. Only 20 per cent comes from our intelligence quotient (IQ). Emotionally connected pupils do better academically, and have lower rates of violence, bullying, vandalism, anxiety and depression.

As babies we are dependent on our carer(s) to 'regulate' us with care and attention, soothing or stimulating us as the need arises. This eventually internalises an ability to self-regulate. Regulatory abilities are the foundation of well-being. Without them we remain distressed and unable to make full use of our intelligence. Most parents and staff want to provide the best opportunities for their children. Let's get emotional education right, and we'll be well on the way.

The purpose of emotions

Within our lower brain, we have rage and fear circuits. When triggered by perceived or actual threat, we are motivated to action, to protect ourselves through fight, flight or freeze. In the primeval world, emotional reactions were survival tactics. All feelings have the capacity to motivate and inform, and are crucial to our safety and continued existence.

Sadness and crying trigger care and comfort from others. Later in onset, social emotions such as sympathy, embarrassment, shame, guilt, jealousy and pride are important for moral development. All the higher cognitive emotions tell us something about how we are relating to others. Understanding our emotions – emotional intelligence – is key to improving our relationships.

Socialisation of emotional development

Without empathy, the most social of feelings, the world would be a pretty dire place to be.

Without empathy, the most social of feelings, the world would be a pretty dire place to be. We need others to respect our right to be safe physically and emotionally. To become a human being who can truly 'feel into another', the infant needs to have someone soothe and respond to the ebbs and tides of their own emotional flow.

Studies show that despite childhood adversity, if a relationship in a child's life provides ongoing emotional support, they can go on to build caring relationships with others. Even victims of poor parenting can succeed and rise above it if a significant carer – particularly in their early years – supports them.

While we'll look at the structure of the brain in detail in Chapter 2, it's important to note here that the circuits of the higher social brain are housed in the neocortex. It's the last part of the brain to gain anatomical maturity, and neural habits can be reframed. The restorative justice process – involving the perpetrator and victim of a crime – succeeds because it awakens and reconnects empathy. To develop empathic skills, positive relationship experiences are essential.

Social Intelligence is much more than empathy
The 3 areas of Social Intelligence are:
1. Art of relating
2. Capacity to negotiate, resolve and be a great team player
3. Capacity for compassion and concern.

Margot Sunderland, *The Science of Parenting*

Gender differences

Noreen Wetton would say: 'We're wired up differently.' We appear to have lost appreciation of the differences between genders. I am continually fascinated by the intensity of feeling and rich emotional language boys convey through drawing and the written word. Girls articulate readily in circle time; boys remain more reticent. Perhaps the anonymity of Draw and Write allows boys to express feelings?

UK and American studies show poorer emotional literacy amongst boys than girls, although boys find it easier to express anger. Most professionals consider anger a 'secondary' feeling, fear being the primary emotion. Do we cringe at boys whimpering in pain, or girls bellowing out in anger? Do we permit feelings in boys that we dislike in girls? If so, we handicap both genders. We need to be mindful of the part we play in accepting children's right to experience and manage feelings common to humankind.

The corpus callosum plays a part in the difference in ability to manage feelings between boys and girls. This 'corridor' runs between the two hemispheres of the higher frontal brain, helping to connect feeling and thinking capacities. Slower to mature in boys, it gives girls the advantage in talking about feelings.

Genders have different biochemical responses under stress. The female brain produces more oxytocin than the male. She seeks a friend to talk to and be calmed by. In men, andogens (male hormones) suppress the calming effect of oxytocin; and oestrogen, the female sex hormone, enhances it.

Women manage stress by seeking companionship, men by going it alone and seeking distraction. Could we allow boys, therefore, some distraction first to destress, then discuss later? Should we encourage girls to talk things over with a friend first, then come back to us?

Cultural diversity in emotional expression

The anthropologist, Paul Ekman, demonstrated that all humans share hardwired emotions: joy, distress, fear, surprise, anger and disgust. The related facial expressions are recognisable across all cultures.

Social or higher cognitive emotions include love, pride, embarrassment and shame. Guilt, jealousy, and envy are also universal, but are triggered and expressed differently by different cultures.

Life circumstances

Sometimes, children are faced with challenging life circumstances such as bereavement, divorce and mental health problems at home. Some children do not tell anyone they are unhappy or scared, and their anxieties, left alone, often get worse. Freud observed 'they proliferate in the dark'. These unaccompanied fears will reveal themselves as phobias, poor concentration, clumsiness, bedwetting and acting out of context.

We have no choice about genetics or many of life's circumstances, but parents and teachers do have choice over how we relate to children. We are in a position to give or seek the emotional support trying times call for.

The very high incident of mental ill health, loneliness, suicide and depression: these are the fruits of inadequate care for children.

John Bowlby

Chapter 2
New science and old theory

We now have the technological capacity to measure and quantify brain activity and emotions. Biochemicals involved in emotional response have been identified. Ironically, as we learn more about how human interaction shapes the brain and the impact of this on our emotional and social development, we are becoming less social.

Many families no longer sit down for a meal together regularly, club membership continues to drop, many children don't play outdoors or mix and mingle. Lost is the opportunity informal play offers. In 2007 a new UK secondary school was built without a playground.

We create one another.

Daniel Goleman

The triune brain

The brain comes in three major interconnected parts. We are born with the lower brain fully intact, and the remaining connections make it work as a whole.

- ❍ The lower, reptilian or primitive brain is instinctive and automatic.
- ❍ The mammalian, limbic or mid brain is where emotional reactions develop and memory is housed.
- ❍ The higher neocortex or prefrontal lobes give us our unique human thinking capacity.

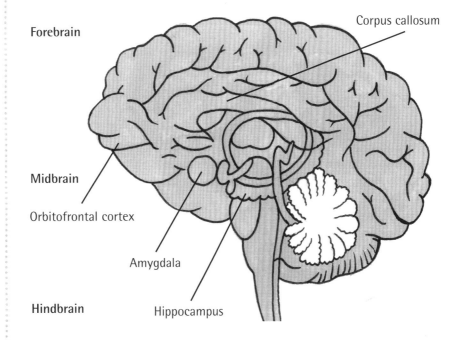

The neocortex is 85 per cent of brain mass, and wraps around the older mammalian and reptilian brain. It comes unwired and we help hardwire it. This is where we can really have an impact on children's emotional capacity.

Lower reptilian brain: Controls heart beat and survival instincts such as when to breathe, eat and sleep. It registers fear, actual or not, within less than a second and sends a message to release adrenaline to ready the muscles for flight, fight or freeze. By building a higher brain that can calm these primitive impulses, there is great potential for us to have an impact.

Mid brain – mammalian brain: Also in higher primates such as monkeys, it governs social behaviour and activates rage, fear, separation distress, seeking, care and play, and in adults lust. It enables mammals to bond and form close relationships.

Amygdala: Housed in the mid brain. It triggers strong emotions that without support from the higher rational brain may fire inappropriately with an urge to fight or flee.

Hippocampus: The central organ for learning and new neural pathway connections. It holds a working memory of new information and converts it to long-term memory, and is vulnerable to emotional distress. This is related to the hormone cortisol.

Neocortex

The higher brain is much slower to develop and operate than the instinctual lower brain. As neural pathways connect, the orbitofrontal cortex, the part most responsible for managing impulses, enables the child to read accurately and respond to emotional cues calmly. New pathways from the higher to the limbic brain are referred to as top-down pathways, which are experience dependent.

Within the neocortex are two hemispheres, the left and right brain. The left is linear and logically inclined – words, language and detail are its forte. The right is more creative, visual and imaginative. Left and right brain integration is fundamental to developing empathy, compassion and concern.

Corpus callosum: Between the mid and higher brain, it links the left and right hemispheres of the neocortex. Through attunement to a child, we strengthen this bridge.

Getting connected

Hardwiring of the brain begins about two months prior to birth, when the foetal brain begins to make connections among its billion brain cells. During the first eighteen months we experience the most rapid brain growth. Reliant on adults to regulate feelings of distress or contentment, the infant adapts to fit their environment. Depressed mothers are likely to have babies who adjust to low stimulation and lack of positive feelings; agitated mothers may have infants who become overaroused or switch off completely to cope. Children will come into class with a pattern already set in motion. Fortunately the brain remains plastic for most of childhood, so there is hope of awakening a new way of being in the child.

Hardwiring of the brain begins about two months prior to birth, when the foetal brain begins to make connections among its billion brain cells.

The baby is an interactive project not a self powered one.

Sue Gerhardt

Use it or lose it

By 3 years of age, practically every brain cell has a connection with another. A refining process starts to cull some of these connections by ignoring the weakest.

Around the age of 7, this pruning slows down, but it continues until the late teens, by which time we will have lost almost half the connections we had when 3. The lost neural connections are almost impossible to revive, but we can strengthen the surviving ones. The more we use a neural pathway, the stronger it gets. Daily interaction with the world governs the way the brain stores information. In effect, we file away learned cues and responses. If I cry and I'm comforted, hungry and I'm fed, I file positive memories. I internalise that the world is a caring and responsive place.

Our minds emerge and our emotions become organised through engagement with other minds, not in isolation.

S. Gerhardt

All is not well if I am raised in a frightening, cold environment. My filing system will consist of distancing and rejection-coping tactics, building an internalised belief that the world is an unhappy and hopeless place.

During the pruning process the emotional limbic and primitive brains are the stronger force. The child is at the mercy of these without support. They may be overwhelmed by a sudden flood of emotion. It's not intentional naughtiness, but a biological reaction. Not helping children with big feelings leaves them overreactive. We all see children who react first, and think a little too late.

Margot Sunderland stresses that if children are left too long, too many times, to manage on their own, with no other support later in life, the hardwiring becomes deficient. Children may be stressed for days or weeks, resulting in clinical depression.

All children are a work in progess. They are dependent on adults to calm them so that the necessary connections can be made in their own minds and internalised as an ability of their own. Although it's not easy to create new pathways as we get older, adolescence opens a window of opportunity, and with loving support, it's never too late.

Chemical cocktail

Let's take an overview of the biochemicals that have significant roles in our emotional well-being.

Each of us has his or her own ... finest drugstore available at the cheapest cost – to produce all the drugs we ever need to run our body and mind.

Candice Poet

Sympathetic nervous system: This brings about a state of arousal and awareness, priming us for protection or motivation. When overactivated, too many stress hormones are released.

Imagine being asked to do something you really dread – for many, it's public speaking. You have to get up in front of a scientific audience and explain all about neuroscience. Can you feel the adrenaline kick in, the heart rate pump, the breath shorten? This is your sympathetic nervous system in action.

Parasympathetic nervous system: This brings relief and rescue.

Opioids and oxytocin: Soothing and calming. Although oxytocin is gone in moments, a steady flow is activated through touch. A hug, embrace or friendly pat, or even an affectionate word, can ease and lower arousal. Touch is the greatest source of regulation for babies, fostering bonding between mother and child.

When opioids flow, we have a general sense of well-being and security. Psychological strength is linked to opioids being strongly activated in the brain. These boosters of contentment can assist us in rising above our worries and anxiety. If we're not touched kindly, or if harsh words hurt, the benefits of opioids are blocked. Recall images of abandoned Romanian orphans rocking themselves in an attempt to self-soothe.

A profoundly positive outcome of activating opioids in children is that it reduces the urge to fight.

Serotonin: Often thought of as the happy hormone is a mood stabiliser. Low levels may result in impulsive behaviour, low or bad moods, and getting upset or overanxious. It can be activated by having fun together, laughter and even mild exercise.

Cortisol: A biological fuel for metabolism, in appropriate amounts and at the right time it helps regulate the immune system and mobilises the body in emergency. Too much, though, and we're in a risky condition of vigilance and overreactivity.

We can't determine what circumstances the children we care for face, now or in the future, but we can affect how they manage them.

Wired to connect

Unless their hearts are already hardened through self-preservation, children will offer up apology and condolence when they've done wrong. Accept with grace the child's attempt to reparate. If you're still cross, defer your response with something like 'I'm glad you're apologising, but I'm still cross now. Let me calm down first' and come back to the child so you receive them authentically. Likewise, compose yourself before apologising to a child.

Nature versus nurture

Another shift in scientific thinking to keep in mind is that genetics does not play as much of a part as previously thought. The basic hardwiring is nature–genetic, but how this gets played out is nurture. Environment and relationships set the expression of many genes.

Never doubt then that as a teacher, you are paving the way for a better neural connection, stashing stores of positive life qualities into the folders for empathy, responsiveness and optimism.

Key relationships can gradually mould certain neural activity. In effect, being chronically hurt and angered, or being emotionally nourished by someone we spend time with daily over the course of years, can fashion our brain.

Daniel Goleman

Read *Inside I'm Hurting* by
Louise Michelle Bombers
(Worth Publishing, 2007)

Attachment

Secure attachment sets a child up to expect the best. Through the care of a
primary attachment figure – usually the mother – they understand that the
world is a safe and good place. Relationships are rewarding and even if things
go wrong, there is help at hand. Cooperative and kind, these children can give
out some of the positive experiences they've internalised. They may need help
with identifying and expressing emotions, but are unlikely to come unstuck
because of this, and can show resilience in the face of adversity.

Be aware of pupils who may not have secure attachment. They are likely to have
difficulty in managing not only their own feelings, but your well-intended offers
of support.

If in doubt, talk it out

In therapy much of the work involves offering attached parenting through a
reparative relationship. Some children will always need more than you will ever
be able to offer in the classroom, and should be referred for play therapy of some
kind. If you have any concerns at all about the child's safety, talk this over with
a colleague and follow the school's child protection guidelines.

Use the computer analogy for the brain

Ask children:

What qualities does it take to wire a complicated and very precious computer? Whom do I have to go to when
I've blown a fuse? At school, at home? What qualities do we need to practise in the classroom so to prevent our
computers going haywire, freezing, or having a melt down?

Bring in a mouse trap that triggers when a stick comes near it. Ask the children what we need to make the
classroom a safe place so we're not all trigger happy.

Do we ever have 'fall-outs' for no reason? What can we do about it?

Can we spot when we're trigger happy? What can we do about it?

Agree on a class signal that can act to calm the amygdala (e.g. 'Calm the storm'.)

Make a display, with pictures, of interactive repair. Include 'How I can come back to my comfort zone through
helpful self-talk', 'How I can help someone back to their comfort zone by what I do or say'.

Chapter 3
The emotionally calming adult

*A person becomes an
I through a You.*

Martin Bouber

Children don't require us to be happy, glowing people all the time, but being approachable helps. We won't be approachable if we're frazzled, worn out and overwhelmed by curriculum pressures and a poor work–life balance.

What does it take to make us approachable, emotionally calming adults able to model emotional competence?

Staff morale and emotional well-being

More UK teaching staff suffer occupational stress and burnout than members of any other helping profession.

Within education, there is no formal procedure for team building or boosting staff morale. That often happens through the camaraderie of the staff room or on an *ad-hoc* basis. Happier staff means less absenteeism and a more productive workforce. We are more resilient to the demands of the job, and more likely to respond with empathy to children's highs and lows.

Read *Turn Your School Round* by Jenny Mosley (LDA, 1993)

Jenny Mosley's QCT model of positive behaviour starts at the top. If you want to esteem children, focus on the adults who care for them. We need to raise staff morale through personal and collective care plans, and to keep a check on mental health and our most valuable resource, staff energy. In all of Jenny's books, you will find advice about this. I am especially aware of the value of the quick fix – the Golden Moment – a time of pure sensory pleasure. For a short time we go back to the senses in order to awaken the spirit, and lift ourselves from mundane day-to-day existence. We recharge our batteries and regain the spark.

When working in a kindergarten in New Zealand, in a four-hour morning session, I used to struggle to finish a cup of tea in the presence of thirty pre-schoolers and two staff. I decided to take in my Golden Cloak, a square of gold lame. I used to drape it over a chair. I would sit in surveillance on the chair with my tea, in my Golden Moment.

When I sat with a Golden Hoop in front of me, this was an invitation to the children to stand inside it to entertain me with jokes or good news stories. The little ones would clamber in, saying 'Oh Anna-Michele – you're a Golden Girl!' I had 3 minutes 37 seconds of entertainment, and we all had an uplifting serotonin boost from the absurdity of it all.

As a staff team, we need to be proactive. How do we look after ourselves and each other? When a situation becomes challenging or overwhelming, as all too often happens, a cascade of stress chemicals such as cortisol and adrenaline can tip us over the edge. Too much cortisol means our immune system is lowered. Before we know it, someone is off work, ill. While mood-lifting interactions alone will not abate stress, they are useful inhibitors.

Being one page ahead

One of the requirements of training in psychotherapy is to undergo therapy yourself. The trainee experiences a reparative relationship first hand, and also reflects on what emotional baggage they carry. That helps them to forestall potential harm and to recognise where they may have difficulty in supporting a client's emotional growth.

There is little time for professional development in this area, and many teachers are uncomfortable about using some of the more sensitive lesson plans offered by SEAL. Like children who struggle to find a language for their feelings, they don't know the words and they don't want to get it wrong.

Not all of us have had secure and happy childhoods. Many of us will be challenged by suffering and anxieties. How we feel about feelings will impact on our ability to support children.

Ask yourself if:

- ❍ you don't want to know about or have difficulty with or an aversion to certain feelings
- ❍ you judge some feelings as more positive or negative than others
- ❍ you are unnerved by feelings when expressed by others – e.g. by crying
- ❍ you ignore or avoid emotion in yourself or others
- ❍ you have feelings you can't contain or become overwhelmed by
- ❍ you still need help with feelings
- ❍ you perpetuate the image of having a stiff upper lip
- ❍ how you handle feelings might affect your ability to recognise or handle a child's feelings?

Emotional competence is a journey, not a destination. Don't fret if you get it wrong sometimes. Plod on. Create a cohort, perhaps via the Internet, of like-minded souls.

Antidote promotes emotional literacy for all – read their newsletters at www.antidote.org.uk/who/newsletter.html. Instead of giving yourself a hard time when you have not quite managed to be the epitome of graciousness, remember that we teach best what we need to learn most.

'Good enough' parenting

I shall borrow from Donald Winnicott, the paediatrician who created the concept of 'good enough parenting'. We're not seeking perfection, but rather working towards positive regard and attunement to children's emotional endeavours. High warmth, low criticism, should be the guiding principle for an emotionally healthy environment in which to raise children. That allows for human error.

I often hear my mother remind me 'We are all flawed.' Certainly, we get it wrong from time to time, despite our good intentions. Misattunement – responding in a way that does not connect with what the child really means or is feeling – is

Read *Becoming Emotionally Intelligent* by Catherine Corrie (Network Continuum, 2003)

Would you like a tissue?

No, I'm fine, thanks.

An African elder, when asked, 'What makes a good man?', replied: 'One who laughs, cries, and protects – and does each when needed.'

Read *Words that Work* by Frank Lunzt (Hyperion, 2007)

Parents can affect the chemistry in a child's brain to such an extent that, for the most part, their stream of inner thoughts will be self encouraging rather than fraught with self criticism.

Margot Sunderland

endurable if balanced by interactive repair. Return to the child, make up and apologise, or just give our full attention at another time when we can be more emotionally present.

Dr Frank Lunzt states there are four stages to an apology that is really credible, sincere and allows us back into the fold:
1. Acknowledge the error: 'I made a mistake.'
2. Express remorse: 'I'm sorry.'
3. Ask for forgiveness: 'Please forgive me.'
4. Make reparation and show an intention to change: 'Let me make it up to you.'

We could encourage children to use the same process with classmates.

Working with parents

Most parents want to do their best by their children. They may not have had enough help with their own feelings to be effective. By working in partnership with them, we offer the child a better chance of cohesion.

Creating a warm and positive ethos

What would I find out about your school from the minute I came in the door? What do children learn about managing the intricacies of human relationships from the way in which staff, pupils and parents and the wider community interact?

For many years, I have been a visiting educational consultant, and I do some supply teaching too. I am always heartened by the schools that welcome me, furnishing me with a timetable, showing me which cup I can use, introducing staff who can be called upon. Welcome and inclusion for all is a sign of emotional intelligence.

Schools need to be safe and inviting for both adults and children. Do all have access to listening systems that will address their concerns and allay their fears? Proactive anti-bullying, positive behaviour and play policies should be seen to be in action. Good practice around diet and exercise is a sign of emotional well-being too.

Creating a secure base in the classroom

Attachment theory stresses the importance of having a secure base to return to. The more a child can depend on their primary care-giver for safety, the more able they are to venture out. By providing a safe haven within the classroom we offer the opportunity for children to extend themselves beyond their comfort zones.

... all of us, from the cradle to the grave, are happiest when life offers us a series of excursions, long or short, from a secure base.

John Bowlby

A number of our moods come to us via our interactions with others. Positively resonant relationships give us a daily dose of emotional vitamins, sustaining and nourishing us. Just by fashioning our face into a smile we can lift our mood and start the serotonin flowing. Start the day with a smile – it's truly infectious!

We have the responsibility of being up to the job, and some self-regulation goes a long way. Is my mood conducive to a warm and happy atmosphere? How do I need to prepare myself emotionally before the start of the school day and after a break?

Do I have:

○ a thought ready to calm me – especially for when others wind me up

○ a quietening technique – rain stick, tambourine (much better than a shrill voice)

○ a signal for children to use if they feel the classroom is becoming too noisy or distracting

○ a time-out zone furnished with an egg timer, so anyone – including staff – can sit out for a minute if they can feel themselves getting a bit 'trigger happy'

○ rules, routines and classroom understandings visible, giving predictability and allowing children to begin to moderate their own and each other's behaviour

○ a way of preventing boredom, and consequential stress?

Good primary practice is all high drama, and low cunning!

Noreen Wetton

Opt for change every now and then to reawaken the senses – such as songs or music to change mood.

Have up your sleeve a host of games – energisers, icebreakers and calming activities – to aid concentration and move on low-level disruption.

Have a good news time: tell a good tale, report on progress towards class targets, try out slogans for promoting self-esteem. Find a way of opening and closing the day positively, such as a round, a story or a calming ritual.

Read:
Better Behaviour Through Golden Time by Jenny Mosley and Helen Sonnet (LDA, 2005)
Using Rewards Wisely by Jenny Mosley and Helen Sonnet (LDA, 2006)
The Science of Parenting by Margot Sunderland (Dorling Kindersley, 2006)

Boundaries

We all need to know when to contain certain states in the interests of safety, respect and social decorum. Validating a child's feelings doesn't mean we agree with them, nor do we always condone their mode of expression. We can pre-empt misbehaviour through boredom by providing sufficient stimulation. Understimulation is registered in the brain as stress. Alleviate this with physical movement – games, energisers, Brain Gym®. Or try a literal shake down: Pilates roll down to touch toes, a huge yawn, a massive sigh and shoulder roll. Or lead a beanbag cheer – throw one in the air, all shout out, and the instant it touches the floor all stop.

Discipline and warnings

Boundaries offer emotional safety and predictability, and help get us back on track when we have erred from or crossed the line. Whatever system your school uses, ideally you are all singing from the same song sheet. Take a positive praise approach: catch them being good. Reward them accordingly.

Withdrawal of privilege has been found to be the most effective form of discipline.

Chapter 4
Classroom techniques

Draw and Write

I like to start subject work with the Draw and Write method pioneered by Noreen Wetton. It provides insight into pupils' changing perceptions by starting where they are at. You become able to identify and target areas of knowledge and perceptions that need reinforcing or rethinking.

The procedure consists of an invitation to draw a picture relating to a given scenario, followed by writing about the drawing. With younger children you may decide to do this over two sessions. Pre-writers can do Draw and Scribe – you will need helpers to write down their responses. The children's pictures are illuminating, and information is obtained from their written statements. The drawing is a non-threatening way of introducing the topic that gives children time to sort out their thoughts. There are a number of Draw and Write activities in the later chapters of this book. The procedure for each of them is as follows.

Materials needed: Pencils and appropriate worksheets. Do not offer erasers and coloured pens.

Suggested preamble: Use something on the following lines.
Today we are going to have a drawing and writing survey of your views. There are no right or wrong answers. It's your ideas that are wanted, so draw quickly and write quickly. You won't colour in your pictures, and stick figures are fine. Don't write your name on your work.

Leave room for writing around your picture. Use thought bubbles to show what the person you draw is thinking, but might not be saying. Use speech bubbles to write what they might say. Use the words 'I feel ...' to describe how they are feeling. You will also write down what the person is doing, and you may write 'I don't know' as an answer.

Use your own spellings – no dictionaries or word books. If you need someone to write something for you, put your hand up and they will come and write what you whisper to them – we don't want to share our ideas. They'll act as your scribe.

When you have finished drawing and writing, put your pencil down and look this way so I know you have finished.

I usually ask the children to repeat the instructions before we start. Keep reassuring them that it's OK to write 'I don't know.'

The rules: Explain that there are some rules.

◉ We won't be talking to each other while we are drawing and writing

◉ We won't be looking at what other people are drawing and writing

◉ You won't be asking me any questions.

Rounding off: At the end of the activity you may want to give the children a little time to finish off their pictures, but do not let them talk and share ideas.

Do thank them for their work, and promise them feedback. Praise them for their efforts and cooperation. Reassure the children that if they need any help with their feelings, you are available to talk to them. You could give a time and place for that. Do look over the work soon so if any follow-up is necessary it is attended to. If you find some work raises concerns, such as a child's safety, seek out a colleague to discuss this with and if necessary take further action in accordance with your school's policy. Although the work is anonymous, you may recognise who it belongs to. Don't value confidentiality over a child's safety.

Children at play are not playing about, their games should be seen as their most serious minded endeavour.

Michel de Montaigne

Play and the arts

A classroom that wants to foster emotional literacy will offer opportunities for children to play – alone, together and through the expressive arts. We must continue to promote the use of arts and play as essential components to building a child's emotional intelligence. The advances of a technological age and academic drive have brought a decline in the ancient arts of dance, song and play. The cost is impoverished imagination and hampered social skills in children. We need to redress this.

The Italian pre-schools of Reggio Emilia in Italy are attracting attention. Village parents who suffered at the hands of the Nazis wanted to raise children and adults who would be more able to resist injustice. To create strong, empathic adults, they start with the child's learning environment, based on aesthetics, play and relationships.

Our intention is clearly to help children search for and discover parts of their world that may risk remaining hidden. Moreover, we want to be sure that the desires, interest, intelligences and capacity for enjoying and seeking – which are a child's inborn resources – do not remain buried and unused.

Loris Malaguzzi

If we utilised more concepts from best early years practice like this, we would go a long way in supporting and redressing children's emotional development throughout their school years.

Neurobiology of play

Play and the associated seeking help us venture forth with curiosity into the world. A sense of inquiry enables us to follow dreams, pursue goals, produce ideas, be involved in joint ventures and motivate ourselves. As adults, when the play system is embedded we can adopt a creative (as opposed to an artistic) approach to our work and daily lives, we are fun to be with, and we have that stress-busting skill often seen on job specifications, a sense of humour.

Physical interactive play between children also has natural anti-stress benefits, reducing tension with potent doses of opioids. This enhances the emotional regulation capacities in the child's higher frontal lobes, helping them to manage their feelings better.

Play is serious, purposeful business ... through which confusions, anxieties and conflicts are often worked through ... Through the safety of play every child can try out his own new ways of being ...

Violet Oaklander

For optimum development, the left-brain verbal operations need to be well connected to the right brain's information capacity via the corpus callosum. The process of putting feelings into words seems to enable brain integration. We begin this process with what I call body talk – hence early years emphasis on sensory play and exploration. These activities free the mind to regulate both the body and emotional arousal. Brain Gym, singing and arts are important because they help to build the road between the brain hemispheres.

The art of play

Play, although innate, needs the right environment. Mary Sheridan identifies four things to ignite the spark. There are many resources available for improving play with children – those mentioned here are grouped according to Sheridan's division.

Playthings

Raw materials that are stage and age appropriate for creative and constructive endeavour. Set out a range of materials each day to stimulate and entice rather than direct or dictate. This free range gives permission to the child in need to regress within a contained time and place. If you run Jenny Mosley's Golden Time, you could make this provision available then. Include such things as these:

- ❍ art materials – for collage; drawing and construction; malleable material (clay etc.); natural objects
- ❍ water trough and sand tray with miniature toys
- ❍ outdoor equipment – balls, ropes, hoops etc.
- ❍ imaginative playthings such as hats, lengths of fabric, puppets
- ❍ craze of the week equipment – Mosley advocates a weekly rota of resources for this
- ❍ games – help children bond through laughter and practise many learning skills.

Solitary play remains the indispensible harbour for the overhauling of shattered emotions after periods of rough going in the social seas.

Milton H. Erickson

Playspace

One of the most productive things to be done in the playground is to zone off spaces to include:

- ❍ comfort zone – beanbags, books etc.
- ❍ zones for active, group and solitary play

Outdoor zoned areas to facilitate:

- ◗ active games
- ◗ team games
- ◗ quiet board games and reading
- ◗ a soft ground area to permit some gentle rough and tumble with adult supervision
- ◗ gardening – fruit and vegetable and wildlife, effectively a living work of art
- ◗ oasis of calm – a place of retreat, with seating and planting, and perhaps sculpture
- ◗ an outdoor platform where children can make a song and dance
- ◗ murals to inspire imaginative play.

Playtime

If children do not get enough socially interactive play, they'll play at the wrong time. Think twice about loss of playtime as punishment, particularly for ADHD pupils. The lack of an outlet for their strong impulses will exacerbate symptoms. Withdrawal of privilege is a more effective sanction.

Use circle time, school councils and assemblies to discuss issues and demonstrate new ideas about playtime. Invite your lunchtime supervisors into these sessions for active listening and quiet explanation.

If you get stuck with wet play, try to include some games to let off steam, lighten the mood and boost serotonin levels. A calming circle time round before class resumes creates an atmosphere conducive to learning.

Playmates

We need only one or two strong friendships to keep loneliness at bay. The isolated child is far more vulnerable to bullying and abuse; finding a way to forge good friendships is paramount to the child's emotional resilience.

Children will go through stages where the nature of friendships changes dramatically. Many schools have formalised systems to ensure that no child is without a friend. Examples are buddy systems, peer mentoring and Jenny Mosley's playground friends. These are beneficial to both the giver and receiver.

Some adults make superb playmates if they are in touch with their 'free child'. This is a recognised playful state in Transactional Analysis that is within us all to varying degrees. We have an adult responsibility to cultivate our 'free child' if we work directly with children.

Sue Jenner talks of 'attending' to the child, rather than directing or teaching. We might say 'That looks like good fun, being a dragon. What would you like me to be or do?' rather than interfering with a demand like 'What do dragons eat?'

"That's a giant peach, James."

Read *The Parent/Child Game*
by Sue Jenner
(Bloomsbury, 2000)

Disciplined forms of enquiry

The arts provide structured forms of play, and participation in the arts gives children the chance to think outside the square, to empathise, to perform. It's what we might call 'the rehearsal of the possible' (Kenneth Robinson). Often considered the domain of either the talented, or quite frankly, in my day, 'the thick', the arts have long been prejudiced as 'flaky', and not of academic rigour. Kenneth Robinson says:

> The arts are not outpouring of emotions.
> They are disciplined forms of enquiry and expression through which to organise feelings and ideas about experiences.
> The need for young people to do this, rather than just give vent to emotion or to have them ignored, must be responded to in schools.
> The arts provide the natural means for this.

Read *The Arts in Schools* edited by Kenneth Robinson (Calouste Gulbenkian Foundation, 1982)

Find time if you can to enjoy playing and working together through a rich and varied arts provision.

Quality Circle Time

I have used circle time for twenty years now. I encourage the use of Jenny Mosley's QCT with its practical and proactive approach to enhancing emotional competence in schools.

QCT is a vehicle for allowing children and adults to get to know themselves and each other; to explore feelings and relationship quandaries; and to celebrate the good and seek support from the peer group. The SEAL curriculum advocates the use of QCT. By giving children the space to explore and develop positive communication skills, we reduce the need for them to act out, play up and continue with that low-level disruption that turns a good day into a disaster.

It's fun. Games bring children together. They can relax and enjoy each other's company without the pressure of having to get it right. Children leave a session with an action plan and a gaggle of helpers to support them.

For more troubled children, and those who've had difficult life experiences, or may be lonely and having difficulty making friends, a small circle of support can facilitate a reparative experience.

Two aspects of the model I make reference to in this book are Bubble Time and Think Books – extensions of classroom listening systems.

Read *They're Driving Me Mad!* by Jenny Mosley and Zara Niwano (LDA, 2007)

Bubble Time is one on one – when you and I are in the bubble no one can interfere. It's time to talk, chat, ponder, share and consult on exciting or worrying matters. You can invite children simply to enjoy their company for a minute or more. Children can plan here with you for circle time, building up their confidence to contribute.

The Think Book provides non-verbal listening, like a private journal. Time is given to draw and write in these. The teacher comments only if invited to do so by the child putting a sticker next to their writing.

A few considerations

Do think about your own energy levels. There are four prerequisites for running QCT.

Positivity: Praise the behaviours you want more of and ignore those you don't.

Good listening: The routines encourage good listening, from both pupils and yourself. A talking object gives the person holding it the right to speak.

Empathy: Allow pupils – or puppets representing pupils – to ask for help from the group. Children share ideas for managing the dilemma presented. Even if a child is simply listening, they learn to feel into others.

Timing: Many schools run circle time on a Friday afternoon – perhaps as an end-of-week treat. Instead, run it early in the week when energy is greater and so you have time to follow up ideas.

Avoid having circle time only when there is a problem. Always have an element of fun and cheerfulness. We want children to go out with positive memories.

Speaking to the young child within a quality piece of literature can cross age, gender and culture.

Children's picture books

Speaking to the young child within a quality piece of literature can cross age, gender and culture.

Well-intended child specialists have been known to write around a specific issue to pave the way for discussion. These books can be tiresome, and the pupils can feel a lecture coming a mile off. Go for books that have humour, word play, rhyme and rhythm, and that depict adult hypocrisy or a human dilemma through a well-constructed metaphor. Illustrations are often so evocative that they could stand alone.

Go for stories like these, as suggested by Baber and Wetton:

- ◗ Stories in which characters are confronted by specific problems or situations. By the end they have learned something about themselves, each other or the world around them.
- ◗ Ones that involve different kinds of problem-solving used by people with different personalities.
- ◗ Stories written so that the quality of the language transports children to another world, time or situation.
- ◗ Stories in which illustrations do more than fill the gaps in the text, by adding a wealth of detail that if written in the text would swamp the storyline.

Always read the story on your own first. You need to know what the metaphor may unleash.

I take picture books into circle time. They are usually not too long, and they lend themselves to following a theme through in one session.

Massage in Schools Programme

In our well-intended desire to give children rights over their bodies and to keep them safe from unwanted or abusive touch, we have become overcautious – or even paranoid. Children need, want and seek nurturing and comforting touch. Through such connection, we activate the oxytocin that bonds and brings us together.

Mia Elmsater and Sylvie Hetu brought their Massage in Schools Programme (MISP) of peer massage to the UK in 2000. It has since become established internationally.

I have piloted MISP as an anti-bullying strategy in seven primary schools that have all experienced profound benefits. We used the Draw and Write technique to illuminate and evaluate perceptions and misconceptions around massage, touch and their impact. That enabled us to decipher what beliefs and behaviours we wanted to reinforce, and what we needed children to rethink.

Not only did pupils gain a sense of calm, stillness, and warmth amongst themselves; they also learned about respect for body space, assertiveness and giving and receiving. MISP is literally hands on, providing a tangible way of exploring feelings – how that stroke feels – and what to do and say about it. It engaged parents and family members, and significantly reduced low-level disruption in the classroom. It was employed as a hands-on tool for conflict resolution by pupils, and it developed more tolerant and empathic relationships between them.

You can read more about this research at www.annamichelehantler.com

A 2-day course will qualify you as an MISP instructor, enabling you to teach children how to use the massage routine. Details for this can be found at www.massageinschools.com

... oxytocin, opioids ... systems appear to be the key participants in these subtle feelings that we humans call acceptance, nurturance and love ... warmth ... these neuro-chemical systems are nature's gifts to us.

Jaak Panksepp

The vision of the Massage in Schools Programme is that every child attending [primary] school experiences positive and nurturing touch every day.

MISP vision statement

Chapter 5
A language for everyday feelings

Social and emotional education is too important to leave to chance. Affective education, as it is sometimes known, is not intended as an interrogation of a child's feelings. Rather it is a recognition that feelings are part of the daily rhythm of life. The more that children are able to name, recognise and think about feelings, the more social their behaviour will be. Children will discover that what we think shapes our feelings and influences our behaviour. This impacts upon others, so as a class we start to work together to create a happy atmosphere, and learn to be sensitive and caring when sad or worrying things happen for any of us.

Anger, fear, sadness and happiness

Both Daniel Goleman and Steve Biddulph identified four main feelings that children need help with: anger, fear, sadness and happiness.

I always think that the children who are in 'loud protest' are healthier than the withdrawn ones at the back of the class. The child of whom you are all too aware knows, albeit unconsciously, that their needs are not being met. The reticent child has almost given up hope. Many children will not understand the psychological ramifications of their behaviour. The question 'Why did you …?' often proves futile. Their behaviour is their best solution for a reality that's just too painful for them to contemplate.

Destructive or creative?

No feeling is bad in itself. Only if its consequences are detrimental to another's happiness – as when children bully and feel good about humiliating the victim – are they damaging. Negative labelling of emotion is not useful; it's how the emotion is expressed that makes it negative or not. Sibling rivalry and jealousy may embitter a child or prompt them to do their best. Guilt and shame may serve as inner reprimands, motivating them to make amends.

Goleman refers to moral emotions such as remorse, shame and embarrassment as social police, keeping us in line with regard to what we do and say.

Neurobiology of emotion

One of the most amazing and reassuring findings I have come across is that Antonio Damasio has demonstrated that 'even just naming the emotion we are feeling can calm the amygdala'.

Big painful feelings activate stress chemicals in the brain and body. Without a language of feelings, these will vent in some way – perhaps undesirably. The child begins to fear feelings rather than valuing them as signals of needs. Our

... keeping a child open to himself, not comforting a child away from his feelings, is the greatest gift of love a parent can give to his child ... to give him himself.

Arthur Janov

Negative labelling of emotion is not useful; it's how the emotion is expressed that makes it negative or not.

job is to help the higher brain develop pathways that will regulate these feelings safely. We need to deal with feelings first – including our own – and then follow with a logical explanation and boundary setting.

John Gottman outlines five key steps to emotional coaching:
1. Being aware of the child's emotion
2. Recognising the emotion as an opportunity for intimacy and teaching
3. Listening empathically and validating the child's feelings
4. Helping the child label the emotions verbally
5. Setting the limits while helping the child solve the problem.

Empathy

A child who has had their feelings responded to appropriately or with good intention will internalise the seeds of empathy. With an interest fostered in their own inner world, and that of those around them, they are able to put themselves into someone else's shoes, to move beyond self-absorption.

They will be uncomfortable when a child is made fun of or picked on. My Draw and Write research on bullying reveals that many react as bystanders, although they know that this is wrong, until they are encouraged to rethink what to do. Turning off empathy unleashes cruelty.

A child who has had their feelings responded to appropriately or with good intention will internalise the seeds of empathy.

Things we can do and say

We can model empathic responses by saying such things as:

❍ Imagine that happened to you …

❍ How would you feel if …?

❍ What made them so angry/frustrated?

❍ What do you think they were feeling before they did/said that?

❍ I imagine it really hurt your feelings when …

❍ Oh yes! That's great. You must be so pleased with yourself!

❍ [As you play together] Dolly is tired; shall we put her in bed?

Do be respectful of the child's resistance. Resistance is there to serve a protective purpose. The child may pick up that you are about to take them on a difficult emotional journey. Match voice tone, volume and language with sensitivity to their mood. Tread carefully, and don't buy into it completely. Acknowledge the difficulty:

❍ I wonder if it feels too scary (painful, worrying) for you to tell me any more right now?

❍ I think it's hard for you to remember how sad you were when your friend went to another school. I wonder what might make it easier for you?

Offer the child a come-back clause – suggest you talk about it at break, that they draw (and write) about it or talk to you (or another appropriate person) privately.

When children suppress feelings, they lose touch with themselves and are left feeling lonely and doubtful. Give them safe ways of expressing what they feel. Tell them there are some matters that are too private for the public domain, but they can be more open in their Think Book and in Bubble Time. Be aware of the difference between emotional safety and suppression of feelings.

Do make observations about feelings. Try not to interpret. 'I notice that ...' is a useful opener that is not invasive.

- I notice that you aren't playing with anyone today. How are you feeling?
- I notice that you are really bouncy today. I wonder if you are feeling excited?

In therapy, we often come back to the simple but potent question, 'And how are you feeling right now?'

Be aware of the safety of metaphor: 'I notice that little pig is under the pile of rubbish. How do you feel, little pig?' Speak directly into the child's play as if identifying with the character – children are prone to do this naturally.

Try to help with closure, and containment of feeling: 'What will you take away from Bubble Time / our conversation / the picture you've shown me?'

Make use of the two Health for Life books, particularly the themes Me and My Relationships and Feelings of Loss and Separation. Another great resource is *Bullying Matters*.

Know when to seek support from colleagues and when to refer a child on.

What children need to know

1. Give them practical methods

Review your listening systems. Do you have Think Books, regular Bubble Time, circle time, a school council? Do you need a small circle of support? Do you need a reporting box for bullying?

You can use Draw and Write (p. 18). Find out if the children need to rethink anything. What would you feel good about reinforcing? Do they know who can give them support? Use the My helping hand worksheet on p. 56.

Monitor the mood: Assess the mood of the class and choose a calming activity or energiser to start the day/session.

Scores: During registration, ask a selection of children to answer with a number from an agreed feeling scale – for example: 1 is really low; 10 is top.

Mood barometer: Make a coloured continuum on a roll of wallpaper or on large cards that you put around the room. Paint it in shades of one colour – e.g. a happy continuum starts pale cream and ends bright yellow. Ask the children to stand under the colour that fits how they feel.

Read *Using Story Telling as a Therapeutic Tool with Children* by Margot Sunderland (Speechmark, 2001)

Read:
Bullying Matters by Margaret Collins and Noreen Wetton (Healthwise Helpline Limited, 2001)

Health for Life Ages 4–7 by Noreen Wetton and Trefor Williams (Nelson Thornes, 2000)

Health for Life Ages 8–11 by Noreen Wetton and Trefor Williams (Nelson Thornes, 2000)

Alphabet of feelings: Choose a letter. Ask them to think of all the feeling words they can that start with it.

That's new to me: Children find a word that is new to them for a feeling. In groups, they look up the meaning, make a body sculpture in pairs, and get the class to guess the word and vote for the best representation. Role-play when someone might feel like that and what to do about it. They could write and draw first-aid ideas for this feeling and add those ideas to a class box.

Show me how you feel: In pairs, children take turns to sculpt their partner into a feeling. A is the sculptor and chooses a feeling to make B into. B is moved into shape, and has to guess the feeling.

Oh what a feeling!: Play a form of charades with emotional expressions such as walking on eggshells, over the moon. Make sure you end on a positive note.

Make my day: Put names into a box. Everyone picks one and becomes the secret angel for the day for the person named. Collect up ideas on cards so children can borrow these if they cannot think of things to do.

Activities

Thinking about feelings: Start with how the children felt when they woke up, when they came to school and just before lunch break. See how feelings change. Help them understand that although we all share a common experience like getting up, we may feel differently about it. Use the worksheet on p. 57.

Tell a good tale: Hope that the children come back after lunch lifting the start of the afternoon with news of all the good things they went out and made happen.

Hot tips and handy hints: Set up a card file (jokes, songs, nonsense rhymes, ideas for random acts of kindness) that they can dip into at appropriate times.

Displays

In chapters 6–9 you'll find ideas for displays. These are general themes to celebrate and enhance children's self-awareness. Here are further ideas.

A sea of feelings: Play with the metaphor. Explore how we can navigate, go with the flow, stay afloat, avoid sinking to the bottom. There are more: crystal clear vision, hidden depths, skimming the surface.

Red flags: Ways of managing feelings that you'd want children to rethink, and those you'd like to reinforce – the life savers.

Emotional change or opposites: A display could be based on 'When I was little I used to feel ... [scared of, suspicious of ...]; now I am bigger I feel ... [brave, trusting] because ...'.

Use the imagination

Here are some sentence openers.

- My colourful cloak of bravery to wrap me in courage
- My shield of armour to protect me from insults and unkind words
- My bottled-up feelings that sometimes bubble over
- My marvellous machine of a body that warns me of danger.

Esteeming ourselves and each other

- I'm so proud of myself because I …
- We love / like / don't like …
- Our first aid for feelings … ideas to heal feelings that hurt …

Circle time rounds

I'm really happy about …
I feel a lot better now because …
I am grateful that …
The best thing about my day has been …

2. Help them move towards feelings

Use the language of QCT:

- When I use my listening skills to hear … I feel …
- When I use my looking skills to watch … I feel …
- When I use my thinking skills to imagine … I feel …

Body talk

Do I make links with what my body tells me about my feelings? As Violet Oaklander says when dealing with a somatic problem such as nail biting, 'give the responsibility of the body back to the owner'.

What's eating you up?: During the morning, after lunch, or when the class is restless, get them to do some movement and reflect on how their bodies feel before and after.

Gather up thoughts on body language: As much as 85 per cent of emotional communication is expressed non-verbally. What are the non-verbals?

Voice: How does tone and volume change a phrase?

Play: Say it Like you Mean it. In pairs, one has to repeatedly say 'No', but vary the tone, volume, gestures and posture. The partner gives feedback on what was most assertive and got the message through. They change roles and repeat.

Songs and music:

Play songs or a piece of music to prompt discussion of feelings.
'What did you do Today to make yourself feel Proud?' – Heather Small
'Show some Emotion' – Joan Armatrading

'Search for the Hero inside Yourself' – M-People
'I did it My Way' – Frank Sinatra or the Gypsy Kings

You could create a particular mood using
'The Four Seasons' – Vivaldi
'Concerto for Harp in F Major' – Bach

3. Give them the experience of being verbally direct

Talk about the language of responsibility to help the children own their feelings. 'I' statements are free from judgement and blame, and help us become our own agents of change.

◑ 'I feel' = self-disclosure, responsibility

◑ 'You make me feel' = confrontation

Put suitable scripts on display in speech bubbles to remind children to speak assertively yet politely:
I feel … when you … What I'd like is … Thank you.

4. Talk with them about feelings

Make sure they understand what empathy and resilience are, what makes them have these qualities, how they show them, what they do when they feel them. Questions for discussion:

◑ What feelings are hard/uncomfortable to talk about?

◑ What feelings are easy/hard to show?

◑ What feelings are easy/hard to recognise in others?

◑ What feelings are easy/hard to change?

Empathy games

Play Imagine: Imagine you do something for or to someone. How will they feel about it? For example, imagine you send a present to Auntie Mel. Imagine how she will feel about receiving it.

Use puppets to tap into children's resourcefulness and empathy through metaphor.

Have a word storm for words to describe feelings.

Children's literature

Read a story with the children. Here are examples that they will learn from.
Jenna and the Trouble Maker – Hiawyn Oram and Tony Ross
What I Like – Catherine and Laurence Anholt
Feelings – Aliki
Dr Xargle's Book of Earth Relations – Jeanne Willis and Tony Ross
Not Now, Bernard – David McKee

Chapter 6
Anger

Unexpressed anger is often at the root of depression amongst teenage suicide victims. Uncontrolled anger is the forceful emotion felt before the trigger is pulled. Inability to manage this powerful and potentially explosive emotion is literally costing us lives.

Anger is often at the forefront of abusive behaviour. It's not surprising that we all too commonly label anger as a 'negative' emotion. But anger need not be damaging or violent.

Role of anger

The ability to express anger healthily, in an assertive and non-threatening manner, is a sign of good mental health and a skill we should encourage. Anger is a natural emotional response to mobilise, protect and help us cope with threats, hurt, violation and frustration. It can allow us to stand up for ourselves or others when undermined, belittled or treated unfairly. However, it needs allies: calm rational thought, self-awareness and empathy; and it needs control tactics.

Neurobiology of anger

Anger is accompanied by physiological and biological changes. For some these are the first sign that they are feeling angry, arriving after the arousal has begun to impact on their physical and mental health:

- ❍ heart rate increases
- ❍ blood pressure rises
- ❍ energy surges as chemicals such as adrenaline and noradrenaline flow
- ❍ cortisol, slow to release and also slow to go, stresses the body and brain more, inhibiting clear thinking.

If prolonged, all this hyperarousal causes undue stress on the body, and impedes thinking and learning capacity in children.

The raw emotional state of anger is first triggered in the lower human brain as an instinctive and impulsive reaction to threat. We are born with this capacity. As the infant grows and is nurtured and soothed in times of distress, the higher brain develops. Its connection is vital to emotional competency in human beings. If we consider a baby, we can witness the primitive brain operating without the neural pathway connections. There is no ability to think about the needs of another — it's an automatic reaction to cry out, scream if necessary, in frustration when hungry, wet or bored. Top-down pathways — neural pathways created to help regulate stress through the ability to think about feelings — elevate us beyond the dictates and primitive rhythms of the lower reptilian brain.

Anger is a natural emotional response to mobilise, protect and help us cope with threats, hurt, violation and frustration.

Our soothing interactions with a child, if consistently applied, help develop the neural pathways the child lacks to be able to regulate their own stress.

Without an internalised emotionally calming presence, the development of the higher brain is impeded and the child cannot think their way out of rage. The brain pumps adrenaline and noradrenaline and the child moves rapidly into a state of hyperarousal. The child is likely to become aggressive — to themselves or another. We will see this in pre-schoolers, who haven't sufficient hardwiring. When we see it in school-aged children, it is likely that something has gone amiss.

Children who commonly feel anger

Some children have great difficulty in managing other feelings not just anger, and become stuck in a pattern of limited emotional response. Anger is quick to surface. They may have become ashamed to admit more vulnerable feelings such as fear, sadness and jealousy. These children differ from those who may simply need permission to express feelings and need help with how to be angry both safely and assertively.

Angry outbursts can cause havoc. These pupils need calming and containment. Early intervention is vital.

My rights end when yours begin

Given help, children may be able to practise skill-based behaviour, to make better choices, rechannel anger and acknowledge their fear. We can support them in internalising a thought process that might go like this: 'Oh, he's just teasing, trying to wind me up. He must be bored or something.'

The angry, hyperaroused child takes the primitive path of fight in what appears to them to be an appropriate response, without the capacity to decipher the difference between these two kinds of response.

Alongside the ability to discern between actual and perceived threat, we need to help bring them to an understanding that their rights end when others' begin. They need to know that even though they have a right to protect their feelings or themselves from being hurt, they don't have the right to hurt another human being.

Out to get you?

On a bad day, in exasperation, we may conclude that some children are deliberately out to inflict pain and misery. Just imagine what it's like to be them — how they feel as they are constantly alert to threat. Many hyperaroused pupils are extremely perceptive to atmosphere and know when and how to push our 'buttons'. For them it's entertaining to watch us screw up and to be taken down.

It's incredibly lonely to be a child who is growing up to alienate those they need most, to interact with their fellow human beings with hostility and animosity, to forge friendships based on fear, berating and bullying and wearing down those who may be their best hope to stop their heart hardening to hate.

Without an internalised emotionally calming presence, the development of the higher brain is impeded and the child cannot think their way out of rage.

Case study

'He got me in a rage, Miss! I had to hit him.'
Brian was 7 years old when he began play therapy sessions in his lunchtimes, no longer safe to be amongst the other children. He was bullying and fiercely aggressive.

For too many times Brian had heard and virtually felt all the blows that his mother was victim to at home. Brian and his siblings lived in an atmosphere of dread. While his violent father had remained in the house, Brian was terrified for his own and the family's safety, yet his outrage with his father remained repressed.

Prior to his recent outbursts at school, Brian had been subdued, and when riled he was sulky – passive aggressive.

When the perpetrator eventually left the family home, Brian's anger exploded. He was constantly in trouble. His teachers were at their wits' end and his mother was guilt ridden. At this point he entered therapy.

If a playmate gave him a certain look, perhaps hit upon an internalised visual memory of the look that preceded his father beating his mother, Brian was deeply affected. Left uncomforted in his distress, he had blocked the painful memory to get through his home life. Any look became a threat to him, and before he knew it, he was entangled in fight.

What was the catalyst for blowing his top after all this time? Perhaps, now that the father had left, Brian felt safe enough to show his outrage at the violence towards his mother. Unable to attack the aggressor, he became one himself.

Brian lacked the thinking capacity of the higher brain to consider how his internal anguish could damage and distance those who were trying to befriend him. He needed someone to see and feel his agony – and did not have the communication skills or the ability to calm himself. If Brian didn't get help, he could become a man just like his father.

Together, the school, his mother and I worked for nearly two years with a variety of strategies to provide a safe and secure environment that would give him the space to explore the immensity of his troubled life. We helped sensitise Brian to his own pain and suffering, alongside offering activities to support his developing frontal higher brain. Eventually he did not instigate fights, could calm himself when agitated, was able to ask for help and show remorse, and could form friendships that were fun and affectionate.

Rewards, praise and consequences were important, as was the use of the creative and expressive arts to role-play and rehearse new skills in managing his anger appropriately. Playtime was reintroduced. Brian had a different play buddy each day of the week to give him moral and practical support if he could feel a mood coming on. There was lots of physical activity and street dance to release years of tension. The school even bought in a yoga teacher for staff and pupils.

It is important to recognise when a child needs more than is feasible within the classroom setting, and when to seek extra help. Brian's capacity to heal was in part due to tremendous courage on his and his mother's part, and to the willingness of the school to prioritise this work. Some of the ideas we used were suitable for a school setting, and you will find out more about them later.

What to do and how to be

Our own frame of mind

At least these children are in loud protest that their needs are not being met. There is a lot of energy in anger. There is hope that we can harness this into life-affirming behaviour.

Be aware of your own emotional education

How we respond to a child's anger is dependent on many factors: the environment and circumstances, our cultural leanings and background, our emotional state, the trigger of anger; our physical health and well-being and own individual perception based on how we have learned to manage and demonstrate feelings. It helps if we reflect on our own learning. These are some questions to consider and talk over with a close colleague or in a staff meeting:

Our own experience of anger
What permission were we given to have angry feelings?
Did this differ from other members of the family?

Our experience of being on the receiving end of anger
Did those with power and authority abuse this with displays of anger that hurt or threatened us or those we cared for?
Did their anger make us unsafe or fearful?

Our contact with influential role models
Were we helped to manage anger positively and healthily?
Were we supported with soothing and comfort when we were frightened by our own or another's anger?
Who gives us calm in our life now?
How can we create more calm in our lives now?

How has anger helped us to make changes in our lives?
Have we been able to make positive use of this emotion?

Can we manage our own, and other people's anger well now?
If not, what stops us?
What do we need to do about this?

If we have a child in our class, or in our care, who is prone to very angry outbursts, and this frightens or panics us, it may be because of unresolved painful memories of our own.

If we are not sufficiently resilient to calm and reassure that child without raising our voice or becoming threatening, or if we turn our back on a highly distressed child, then we need to do something about it.

We may need to apologise if we know we have let them down, or we've lost our temper in response.

Model positive co-parenting

We, the adults, must hold on to the hope for the child that things are going to get better. Do so together. What the challenging, angry child doesn't need is to watch us go under as they strive to divide the enemy and conquer.

Make the out-of-control feelings of any child a whole-school problem to be solved and strategised together. Use staff meetings for help and ideas. Sometimes having colleagues' empathy is support enough.

Ignore colleagues who say 'Oh, but he wasn't like that with me last year.'

Use one of Jenny Mosley's strategies for 'children beyond' – timetabling breaks for yourself, the child and the rest of the class. Here's how it works:

The child concerned goes to Mr Brown at 10.00 a.m. every Tuesday, and to Ms Elliot on Wednesday after lunch. It's nothing to do with behaviour, but a relief for all concerned. Take the breaks early in the week. You'll need to keep the colleagues concerned on your side, so it's best if the child goes into their class in a calm state.

Consult parents or carers to see if the child makes similar angry outbursts at home. Find out how they deal with them and try to work to a consistent pattern of calming. Consider a parenting skills group – for all parents – on managing tantrums and challenging behaviour. If there is no problem at home, maybe the child's anger at school is to do with peer relationships. Is the child being bullied?

Make sure you and your team are looking after yourselves. Have some Golden Moments to help you to be cool, calm and collected.

Benefits of boundaries

Understanding is not enough. A child's distress is genuine, but so may be the pain inflicted on another. If consequences are required, they should follow after the calm, not before. Punishment and reasoning when the child loses it are the least effective intervention at this time.

Children are likely to have full command of language; they will argue back, have an absence of tears and thrive on an audience. If a child is having a drama tantrum, move away and do not give them attention. Do not negotiate. Give clear and firm responses, and avoid confrontation and harsh criticism – this too readily becomes dismissive and shaming or invites defiance.

Keep discipline consistent with your school behaviour policy, and keep parents informed so the child is not disciplined twice for one offence.

Offer the child the chance to make reparation when they are ready. Interactive repair between pupils and staff can prevent long-term hostilities.

Staying cool

When managing a child's angry outburst we can try these:

Take a deep breath. This child needs calm. Our composure will be a model for them.

Use a warm, steady and sincere tone of voice. Do not plead.

Give firm instructions to stop what they are doing if anyone is being hurt or is unsafe.

Use short statements, repeating them if necessary. 'Let him go. Now. Thank you.'

Acknowledge how angry they must feel. 'You seem a bit annoyed with Ashad' won't help if the child had their hands around Ashad's neck. 'I think you are furious with Ashad. So furious you wanted to throttle him' is closer.

If you are the only adult present, comfort and get help for Ashad, while verbally calming the other child. 'I'm going to help Ashad now. Rest and sit down. I will come back to help you soon.' Try a look of reassurance rather than blame.

Don't insist on direct eye contact, especially with boys. This may register in the primitive brain as a threat.

Say things which give containment to the situation:

- ● 'I can see how angry you are right now – it must feel awful for you.'
- ● 'I know you feel like punching Ashad, but it's not OK to do that.'
- ● 'I'm here to help you calm down. It's OK, I'm going to stay with you.'
- ● 'Take a seat, put your hands on your knees [or go into the squat posture with hands on thighs] and breathe slowly, big sighs.' Do it with them so they don't feel silly.
- ● Don't insist on direct eye contact, especially with boys. This may register in the primitive brain as a threat.
- ● Be aware of your body language. Do not tower over the child in an intimidating fashion. Consider if it is appropriate to touch the child reassuringly, to help soothe them. Hold them firmly if this feels right.

Be familiar with the DCSF's ruling on holding children. This states that when all verbal calming has failed, and the child is about to hurt themselves, others or property, firm holding may be necessary. Consult Section 550A of the Education Act 1996 for details. Try firm holding only if you are physically able to do this, without hurting them or vice versa – that will be counterproductive.

Time In

Margot Sunderland recommends time in, away from the flare up. Children can think and talk about what happened once they are calmer, and name the range of feelings, identifying the triggers and their own bodily arousal.

Validate but don't condone: 'I think that when Lana took the ball you felt it was really unfair of her. That made you very angry. But it's not OK to hit Lana for it.'

What children need to know

Violet Oaklander recognises four phases in working with children's anger; the following suggestions are grouped by them.

Read *Windows to our Children* by Violet Oaklander (Gestalt Journal Press, 1989)

1. Give them practical methods

Use the Angry time worksheet on p. 58.

Make this practical and fun. Boost seratonin levels with games, physical activity and sharing good times. Through discussion, help them decide which activities are OK for the classroom, the playground, and with mates after school, at home.

Voluntary time out in the classroom: Create a place where children can take themselves if they feel they are getting close to blowing it. Explain that it is to be used only in dire need and for no more than a set period of time. Have a big egg timer available so the child can watch the sand run through.

Read *Using Story Telling as a Therapeutic Tool with Children* by Margot Sunderland (Speechmark, 2001)

Some of you will feel that there should be nothing to play with here, but at least have somewhere comfortable to sit. I'd include some little toys such as cars and people and a small sand tray, where they can enact their emerging feelings.

Have some malleable materials available. Ideally, a TA or other adult would accompany the child to help them process some of their feelings. They can tell the angry story in the sand and squeeze their feelings out in the dough.

Fast and furious games

- Clapping games are good for left- and right-brain integration.
- Blow It!: Blow balloons up and let them go; blow them up and let them stretch out the mouthpiece to make a squealing sound.
- Use or make African drums – or try empty water-cooler bottles turned upside down. Encourage them to imagine scenarios that reflect anger: they can drum like the sound of a herd of elephants charging, or a mouse having a tantrum. One child could 'tell' a 10–30-second story of anger on the drum, and then get the group to repeat it. Finish with soothing sound – ask the children for ideas: a trickle of water, a sea breeze …

Play a relaxing piece of music: the children can sway together in a circle, or lie down and close their eyes.

Art activities

Malleable materials: Clay, play dough, plasticine and finger paint are all good for cathartic release.

Paint and collage: Consider metaphors within a landscape to represent the troughs and peaks of angry feelings – volcano, forest fire, bonfire. Include a peaceful counterpart: a cascading waterfall, a still pool. Discuss living in the hot and fiery environment without the cooling, calm waters.

Temperature rising: Prepare a range of shades of hot colours that the children can use to identify the intensity of a feeling about a circumstance: pale pink for having to wait in line; scarlet for when my sister goes into my room.

Calming down
- ◗ How to keep your cool wall chart: Gather up ideas and draw faces with speech bubbles such as, 'I like to calm down by …'.
- ◗ Create a cool-down box: Gather ideas on how to chill out. Tell the children they will draw and write about each on a plastic or polystyrene cup to represent an ice cube. They chuck the ice in a box. Whenever they feel the need, they take one out and borrow the idea.

Circle time games
Collect up angry words on cards and put them in a container. The children pull these out randomly and make up a sentence for the feeling.

Change places if … you feel annoyed with people when they … [do not use names negatively]

Let it out!
'How about grabbing this cushion and saying and doing all the things you would like to do with your anger to it.'
'Run like mad to the fence and back – and again – like a raging bull.'
'Take this crayon and draw on the page how big your angry feelings are.'

2. Help them move towards feelings

- ◗ Help children become more comfortable with expressing their anger. Start small, gradually building up to a manageable level. Mirror some of their movements so they are less likely to be embarrassed. You could start by ripping up very tiny pieces of paper, whispering who or what you're angry with, and progress to ripping up large sheets or old phone books and shouting.
- ◗ If I were an angry animal I would be … The child acts out the animal movement and sound – roar like a lion, shriek like a monkey.

Songs and music: Play songs or a piece of music to prompt discussion of the feelings. Here are some ideas:

'Shout' – Tears for Fears

'If you're Happy and you Know it … Stamp your Feet'

Dance and film: Play scenes from a film to initiate reflection:
Billy Elliot – scene where the dance teacher comes to Billy's house about the audition. Be aware of the swearing in this clip – watch it first.

Encourage children to make up movements of their own that express angry feelings.

Watch a clip of the Haka, the Maori war dance.

3. Giving them the experience of being verbally direct

It is easy to fly into a passion — anybody can do that. But to be angry with the right person to the right extent and at the right time and with the right object and in the right way — that is not easy, and it is not everyone who can do it.

Aristotle

Discuss Aristotle's words. Some of us bottle feelings up, developing passive aggressive means of expression such as sulking, letting people down, sabotaging and being noncommittal. If children don't feel able to talk directly to the person they are angry with, there are ways around this. Through rehearsal and practice they may build the courage and acknowledge that they have the right to do this.

Case study

In a kindergarten, I was impressed when I overheard a 4-year-old say, firmly but not unkindly, to another child: 'No!, Stop! I don't like it when you do that.'

The little fellow who was causing the grievance looked him defiantly in the eye and proceeded to ignore this civil yet assertive plea.

Unthwarted, the complainant repeated his request, this time lowering his head to catch his eye: 'Stop it, thank you!' No fisticuffs, pushing or crying. The other child complied.

Rehearsal of the possible: The opportunity may be lost for some children to be able to say how angry they are with an absent parent. However, it is never too late to release these feelings from the body. Some of these techniques will support children who struggle with anger buried deep from long ago. With your presence and by witnessing such expression, children are sometimes freed up from a debilitating dilemma and enabled to move on.

- ❍ Practise and storytell with puppets.
- ❍ Role-play — create scenarios that the children want help with. Have small props to distinguish roles. The removal of these help with deroling.
- ❍ Use hot seating to empower the child with other ideas and strategies for speaking up about their angry feelings.

TV news/broadcast: Make up a news report about a fictional character who gets angry with someone in a public place. The child can express their angry feelings about someone and even to someone, but indirectly so the relationship remains intact.

Letter writing: Write pretend letters of complaint to customer services. Children can write two kinds — one where they say what they like about their annoyance (language permitting) and one which expresses their dissatisfaction but in which they consider the recipient's feelings. Discuss the difference in outcome.

Write a letter to someone you are angry with – one you burn or tear up. Then write one you could send. Ensure that the language of responsibility – 'I language' – is used.

4. Talk with them about anger

Use Draw and Write as a means to encourage them to talk with others about anger. Use the Were you angry? worksheet on p. 59.

Have a word storm for the angry feelings. You may need to add 'that are appropriate for the classroom' or make rules about slang and swear words.

Debate and discuss: Choose topics such as the following.

- You can change how you feel.
- You have a right to be angry.
- Both boys and girls feel angry.
- There are different things you can do with angry feelings – some safe, some not so safe.
- You can't act on all your violent and murderous feelings.
- My right to be angry, and my rights end where yours begin.

Children's literature about anger and calming

Hug – Jez Alborough
The Bad-Tempered Ladybird – Eric Carle
Mine! – Hiawyn Oram and Mary Rees
Where the Wild Things are – Maurice Sendak
Benjamin and Tulip – Rosemary Wells
The Witch in the Cherry Tree – Margaret Mahy and Jenny Williams
The Big Big Sea – Martin Waddell and Jennifer Eachus

Chapter 7
Fear, worry and anxiety

We explain children's fears away rather than accepting them. Consequently children push down their fears.

Anxiety has always played a crucial role in our survival, but is less essential now than in primitive times. Our fears get in our way. Society dictates that we do not show cowardice. We explain children's fears away rather than accepting them. Consequently children push down their fears.

Social rejection is our most common form of anxiety. Rejection resonates as a primal threat, harking back to times when to be abandoned or outcast by the tribe meant imminent demise.

When children are bullied and others become bystanders, they become separated from the social radar. Ostracism registers in the same part of the brain as physical pain, affecting the capacity to think clearly.

For some children whom we support, a deeply anxious state is rooted in early relational stress that makes them prone to worry, anxiety and – in extreme cases – phobias. With interactive repair, the child reinstates their confidence in themselves and close relationships.

Children will present with a range of anxious behaviours in an attempt to allay their own fears and to conceal from others their fear of being humiliated or, worse, being unprotected. Fear is strongly somatic and many symptoms appear within the body: stammering, tummy aches, bed-wetting, nail-biting.

Phobic thinking

Phobias develop when a child attaches fear to an object to avoid an alarming situation. This may be associative – the child is afraid of spiders, and has a past experience that terrified them when one ran over them in bed at night. A phobia may be symbolic – the spider represents another danger, such as fear of someone coming into their bed at night.

The child is desperate to avoid being retraumatised. They are in need of support that is often beyond the scope of the classroom, but don't underestimate your ability to allay children's fears through your calm and consistent support.

The culprit is an over active Amygdala, one that sends surges of panic in mistaken reaction to cues vaguely reminiscent of the original trauma.

Dan Baker

Neurobiology of fear and anxiety

We know our lower brain is primed with two primary survival hormones – cortisol and adrenaline – to gear our bodies for flight or fight. This was helpful millions of years ago, but less practical today.

We can't always be sure we'll hear the voice of reason. However, the fear system can be overpowered by the neocortex, which can send messages of comfort and confidence to the rebounding amygdala to quieten and calm the nervous system.

If the parasympathetic system is blocked and we have no one to calm our arousal levels, the cardiovascular system will remain activated. Even if the fearful feelings are suppressed, anxiety festers within. These results are seen in children who are hypervigilant.

I'm too shy

It has been argued that shyness is innate. Temperament is certainly genetic, but neuroscience has shown that social experiences and our diet power the genomic on–off switch. A predisposition to shyness will be affected by how effectively the child is encouraged and cajoled to move out of it.

The child may have a tendency to respond in social contexts with heightened anxiety, self-consciousness and reticence, but we can do much to reassure them that the world is a safe place.

One of the important interventions to reduce timidity in children is to encourage eye contact. If they avoid this, they miss opportunities to read cues from others accurately, and may draw on their own fears instead. Eye contact helps build connections and readiness to receive warmth or willingness to connect.

Shy children need lots of play with other children. We should remind them of enjoyable activities as fear will hamper their memory.

Give shy children advance warning of involvement, and allow props such as puppets to act as a communication bridge. Avoid talking for the child.

Building resilience

When a challenge exceeds our ability, healthy levels of cortisol energise us to take a risk and give it a go, or to forge on and complete a task. If we are too fearful, and have not developed resilience, the way ahead is impeded by anxieties and phobias, and later in life by depression. We need to repeat and practise coping with experiences that are just scary enough so that fear will turn to calm. In that way the neocortex acquires resilience.

One way to do this is to move from 1 to 2 below, and from 3 back to 2:
1. Comfort zone – can do.
2. Challenge zone – will do.
3. Stress zone – shan't do!

Each of us is born with a renewable capability for resilience – the built in power to heal, regenerate, and grow beyond our last known limit.

Karen Reivich and Andrew Shatté

This has implications for teaching – differentiation and acknowledgement of different learning styles is important to stretch children out of their comfort zones, but must not stress them beyond their capabilities.

There's an argument for building resilience by using fairy-tales and happy-ever-after stories. They give reassurance that it will be all right in the end.

What we need to know and how to be

Check that you have what you need to be an emotionally calming adult. Consider a visual aid for yourself in the classroom – something that lifts your spirits. Oxytocin flows when we visualise our loved ones. You could make a display of the people who are important to you, and of things you love to do to create a secure base. The children can join in.

Exercise relieves and prevents anxiety, decreasing the biological stress and fear response. Find a way to have the children engage in movement – especially before tests and high performance tasks.

With anxious children create targets for answering questions in class. One teacher negotiated with a lad to put his hand up with his fist closed, signifying that he didn't have the answer but was practising participation. She could praise his effort without fear of shaming him.

What children need to know

1. Give them practical methods

Games: Ones that are just scary enough:

- ❯ What's the Time, Mr Wolf?
- ❯ We're going on a Bear Hunt
- ❯ Eye contact games – Pass the Smile, Wink Murder, Facial Mirroring

Art activity
The children draw or build a factory with boxes, Lego® or blocks. Place in it all the concerns and worries that children have. The only way to escape the factory is by using a Tell Someone ticket for each worry. Pair children up to talk them over, or let them book time with you.

Guatemalan Worry Dolls can be purchased at Oxfam. These are little dolls that children unload to before they go to sleep, then place them under the pillow. Have a classroom set and let children borrow one.

Shoe-box activities
Get the children to write down things they conceal or have inside them that not everyone sees. They put them in a shoe box representing their secret self.

Decorate a box as a treasure chest. They can put more positive things in it.

The point of crisis, when fear is triggered, is a vital time for the 'teacher' to hold onto thinking, to be non-reactive and to communicate some understanding.

Heather Geddes

What's the time, Mr Wolf?

Time you got a watch.

We cannot escape fear. We can only transform it into a companion that accompanies us on all our exciting adventures.

Susan Jeffers

Displays
The following are ideas for all to contribute to:
- ❍ Things I used to worry about before I knew better
- ❍ The rollercoaster ride of risk and excitement

Circle time rituals
Have a class circle time to review any concerns to go to the school council.
Think of something you want to achieve, make a small target for it – and do a round.

2. Help them move towards feelings
Body Talk: Relaxation and meditation activities to slow breathing, calm the mind and release muscle tension

Lots of body work to 'feel the fear and do it anyway' – walk planks, balance, do body control exercises and yoga postures

Songs and music: Use this to prompt discussion; here are examples:
   'Pick Yourself Up' (performed by Fred Astaire and Ginger Rogers)
   'I Will Survive' – Gloria Gaynor
   'Respect' – Aretha Franklin
   'Don't Worry, Be Happy' – Bobby McFerrin
   'Help!' – The Beatles

3. Give them the experience of being verbally direct
Resilience exercise: – the children discuss these:
- ❍ Comfort zone – three things I'm comfortable to share/discuss
- ❍ Challenge zone – three things I'm not so comfortable, but still OK with
- ❍ Stress zone – three things I don't want to discuss at all

They write the following on speech or thought bubbles:
- ❍ I need some help with …
- ❍ I'm getting better at …
- ❍ Next time I'll do better at …

4. Talk with them about feelings
Worry wart: Discuss what makes your worry wart grow.

Draw and Write: Use the Were you scared? worksheet on p. 60.

Children's literature
Oscar Got the Blame – Tony Ross
The Owl Who Was Afraid of the Dark – Jill Tomlinson
Super Dooper Jezebel – Tony Ross
The Velveteen Rabbit – Margery Williams
The Very Worst Monster – Pat Hutchins
Willy the Wimp – Anthony Browne

Chapter 8
Sadness, loss and loneliness

Sadness is linked to losing those we cherish or not having nurturing relationships. Our most painful losses are deeply and acutely felt. Lonely children may yearn to find a special friend.

Children's experience of loss

During their young lives children will face many experiences of loss. A new nursery, teacher or classroom; the death of a pet, grandparent, or close family member: children will struggle to integrate such things into their lives if they are not supported. Those who have an illness or disability may lose out on inclusion by their peer group. Loss of life as it was, before problems of unemployment, poverty or war, can turn a life upside down. Children name the feelings raised by separation, divorce and blended families as those with which they most need help. Some young souls yearn for a parent they never had – because of abandonment, abuse or lack of emotional presence.

An estimated 40,000 children in the UK lose a parent each year and a similar number lose a sibling. In England and Wales 100,000 children have fathers in prison. Two thirds of marriages end in divorce. Children who lose a parent are prone to depression and anxiety later in life.

The Home Office reports that the biggest group of children excluded at under 9 years of age were all bereaved.

Boys seem more affected than girls by parental bereavement. A ChildLine survey suggests boys are less likely to seek counselling and more likely to act out distress, often aggressively. When children lose a parent they may be so anxious about the survival of the other that they conceal their despair in order to protect that remaining parent. Compassionate attention is required to avoid the child turning their internalised pain into externalised violence and hostility.

Stages of grief
Elizabeth Kübler-Ross was one of the first to identify the process of grieving, regardless of the loss.

Stages of grief
Denial – we're in shock and can't come to terms with what's happened. We ignore the reality or search for explanations.
Anger – the injustice and abandonment of loss is felt.
Guilt – often mind bargaining: 'if only I'd'.
Acceptance – we move on with the loss as part of our lives.

Children may not pass through the stages of grief sequentially and may get stuck. Usually lasting about two years after the event, their reaction may be delayed, prolonged or disturbed. Sometimes there will be a noticeable change in children, especially adolescents, one or two years later.

Children react in a variety of ways. We need to be aware that their symptoms range from anger, tearfulness and confusion to disassociation, and they may get worse. The young child may appear to be OK but they may still be hurting.

An understanding of death as being final is grasped around the age of 5. It is best to prepare children of this age if they face the terminal illness of parent, sibling or friend.

Parental support

A parent may be too overwhelmed with their own loss – or bitterness to support their child. Encourage them to make time for their children – often they are inadvertently neglected. School can be very supportive, designating an 'approachable adult' from whom a child may seek solace and support.

Encourage the parent to share their grief with the child, not hide it. Encourage the parent to alleviate any guilt in the child too: 'I'm sure Lee would have forgiven you. It's not your fault that he died.'

Consoling words can be powerful antidepressants.

Neurobiology of sadness and grief

Loss and disappointment activate pain centres – the same part as for physical pain. This can be overwhelming for children. By acknowledging how hurtful and painful it is, we give some immediate relief.

When we lose someone or something special, our separation distress system kicks in, and chemicals go awry. There is a withdrawal of opioids (our anti-aggressive chemicals) and acetylcholine is released. This chemical naturally supports concentration and alertness, but in high doses it causes extreme agitation, making us prone to angry and impulsive outbursts, poor concentration and mood swings. Children who feel their heart has been broken will harden themselves to this excruciatingly painful opioid withdrawal and become defended with hate.

What we need to know and how to be

Your emotionally calming presence activates part of the parasympathetic nervous system. Your vagal nerve has good tone when you can quieten, comfort and reassure yourself in times of distress. Extend this, either physically or with a warm, reassuring tone, when you talk to the grieving child. Consoling words can be powerful antidepressants. Even if you are lost for words, by being with the child you become a biological ally.

If the child becomes aggressive, let them claim back some personal power by coming up with acceptable ideas for release.

John Bowlby identified the needs of a grieving child as these:

- ❍ information
- ❍ honest and factual answers as and when asked

◐ being able to take part in the grieving process, such as a funeral

◐ the comforting presence of an adult who can reassure them that many things will continue as normal.

What to do

Avoid confusing expressions and concepts such as gone before, departed, gone to heaven. Keep language clear and simple.

Attempt to answer questions immediately, so the child doesn't think deferral implies they were wrong to ask. If you can't answer at the time, let them know when you will.

Keep up regular routines in the school day.

Encourage activities and social networks.

Express your own sorrow for their loss and empathise with their sadness.

Articulate your own feelings. You could add, for example, 'I imagine you might have some of these feelings too, only much much bigger because it was your mum.'

Offer a get-out clause – say 'If you have any feelings so big that you can't concentrate or play well, I'd like you to let one of the adults know so we can help you. Who do you think you might like to go to?' For the more taciturn child consider offering: 'Would you like a code signal that could say it for you?' (e.g.: a pebble or card kept in the pocket to be handed to an appropriate adult when feeling in need of comfort.)

Allow a child physically close if this is part of your existing relationship. Hugs, touches and strokes are reassuring.

Recognise that a child's anger or sense of betrayal can arise at any time – and it's not 'naughtiness', but deferred grief; they may regress emotionally and academically.

Do help to translate child behavioural response into feeling language. For example: 'I'm wondering about your angry outburst over non-uniform day being cancelled. It seems to me you are really angry. Do you think you might be really angry and upset about your mum leaving? That must have been a shock.'

What children need to know

1. Give them practical methods

Encourage expression of their feelings: Use the All better worksheet on p. 61. Develop this by getting them to focus on other people's feelings – see the interview worksheet on p. 62.

Write a letter to the missing person.

Games: These give an opportunity to talk about losing something special.
Hide and Seek
Hunt the Thimble
Use games with random pair activities for the lonely child.

Art activities
Make posters with faces showing the range of emotions evoked by the loss.
Make memory books with photos of special times and places.
Memory garden – draw plans for one, and, if possible, make it real.

Treasure or rubbish: Especially for children who had an insecure or ambivalent relationship. Make a treasure box for the memories they value, and draw jewels on card, write in these and add sparkles. Make a cardboard rubbish bin for the ones they want to get rid of. When the bin is full, throw it away.

Construct a shrine: Use colours and symbols that represent the person's characteristics or memories of them.

Construct a 3D trophy award 'To my best ...': Fill it with trinkets or buttons that symbolise memories.

Make a 'Blue Aid' box: Put cards in it suggesting all the things the child can do in school to help with feelings.

Circle time ritual: Honour the special qualities of that person/time/place.

2. Help them move towards feelings
Encourage them to give emotional expression to their feelings with support.

Body talk: Give them a hug.

If using MISP, invite the child to ask for a massage from a peer.

Play touch games in a circle: e.g. make up movements of the life cycle of a plant, playing them out on each other's backs.

If this is not a usual reaction for this particular child, show them how to release anger by hitting cushions, in sport, or by paint and using clay. Always conclude with a calming reflection.

Encourage quiet reflection: fill the body with light and colour. Name the feeling. Practise deep breathing.

Songs and music: Play songs or a piece of music to prompt discussion of the feelings. Here are examples:
'Waterfall' – The Pretenders
'Cry me a river' – Ella Fitzgerald

'The Long and Winding Road' – The Beatles
'You've Got a Friend' – Carole King
'Tears in Heaven' – Eric Clapton
'Bridge over Troubled Water' – Simon and Garfunkel

Films
Bambi; Meet the Robinsons; My Neighbour Totoro.

3. Give them the experience of being verbally direct
Let them say what they need to the person they need to say it to (that person is not, of course, present).

Use Gestalt dialoguing: Talk as if the person is in an empty chair, or use puppets. Ask: 'If you were able to say anything to them now, what would it be? … What would they say back to you?' Move into the chair or use a puppet to represent the other person. You can do this on paper and have the child draw speech and thought bubbles instead.

Encourage reflection: Make an events calendar with them and talk through the special dates.

Establish a peer-mediation process: For children who have fallen out and need to resolve their differences.

4. Talk with them about feelings
Have a word storm for language of loss.

Discuss the following
- Life cycles in nature and the change in seasons.
- Losing special toys, favourite clothes not fitting any more, having to say goodbye at the end of holidays, end of term.

If children ask you about death and dying, ask them what they think they know first. What personal experience have they of it? Clarify for them the reality (or not) of this. You could use the text in the margin.

Children's literature
Badger's Parting Gift – Susan Varley
Fred – Posy Simmonds
Cinderella
Where's My Teddy? – Jez Alborough
Are you my Mother? – P.D. Eastman
Olivia and the Missing Toy – Ian Falconer
Nothing – Mick Inkpen
Michael Rosen's Sad Book – Michael Rosen and Quentin Blake

We cannot prevent the birds of sorrow from landing on our shoulder. We can prevent them from nesting in our hair.

Old Chinese proverb

No one knows for certain where we go when we die, and people have all sorts of different answers. What we do know is that we'll never see that person (or pet) in the same way again. They won't be coming back. You won't be able to touch them or talk to them like you used to, but you can still do it in your imagination.

Chapter 9
Happiness

The new trend in psychology now is not merely to treat psychosis and neurosis, but to help people feel happy. Happy children are more energetic, persistent, creative, focused and cooperative with other children and teachers.

Happy people are characterized above all else by their connectedness and sociality ... personal relationships are the single most important building block of happiness ... .

Paul Martin

Paul Martin claims that happiness-centred education would:

- ◗ promote a life-long love of learning for its own sake
- ◗ be less preoccupied with short-term measurable assessment
- ◗ place greater emphasis on social and emotional development
- ◗ let children play
- ◗ stop encouraging children to acquire academic qualifications at younger ages.

Happiness is a by-product of certain qualities present in life, not necessarily all at once, but in some abundance. Research shows that good health, good friends and above all good family relationships are key to a happy life.

Contrary to popular belief, levels of happiness are not linked to education, age or monetary position.

Children whose main aspirations centre on money, fame or their own physical appearance tend to have poorer mental health than those who aim to develop close relationships and help others. Pre-teenagers who believe that fame and money lead to happiness are identified as being more vulnerable to depression.

The good news is that we can make ourselves happier. One of the most effective tools for happiness is doing good and charitable concern. We feel better about ourselves and our lot when comparing ourselves with others who are not so fortunate.

Pleasurable experiences generally provide short-term happiness, succeeding as punctuation marks in life, not mainstays. Qualities like optimism, love and courage propel us past pain and enable us to forge relationships that will stand us in good stead for improved health and fulfilment.

Neurobiology of happiness

Happiness is not simply a subjective state. Brain activity can be measured showing that sustained forms of positive feelings are good for us. Happy people tend to have more robust immune systems, less stress (and less cortisol), better recovery rates from illness and enhanced longevity. Our body chemistry responds well to good experiences, blood pressure and heart rate are lower, and we stabilise arousal levels.

The biological circuitry of fear is the greatest enemy of happiness. Our automatic fear response has us hardwired for hard times.

Our evolving neocortex is our saviour. This higher-functioning brain houses intellectual, creative and spiritual abilities to free us from fears that thwart our happiness. Certain activities will bring about a positive change in brain chemistry.

Meditation: Induces reductions in heart rate and blood pressure and can have long-lasting results.

Visualisation: Can directly reframe bad feelings about ourselves.

Humour and laughter: Generate measured reductions in stressful amounts of adrenaline and cortisol. Smiling – preferably genuinely, but even shaping the mouth into a smile – will make us feel better.

Exercise: Increases endorphin output by 500 per cent. A daily 30–45 minutes of cardiovascular exercise lifts and stabilises mood. Even movement for a few minutes can revitalise you. As a class teacher, find ways to keep yourself and your pupils from stagnating behind desks.

Affirmations: Simply saying good things in our head – about ourselves, others or daily life – can calm the nervous system and change moods. Our brain creates language and language creates the brain. Write affirmations on cards, e.g. 'I am enough', 'I am sufficient.'

Music: Songs with positive messages particularly can improve moods.

Winning experiences: To avoid pessimism and lethargy in children, ensure that they have opportunity for learned mastery, not to fail too many times nor to be enforced into a lose–lose situation.

What we need to know

Some children are so full of troubled feelings that they can't simply be 'topped up'. Therapeutic emptying out is needed before these children can access awe and wonder in their world.

Things to say
Yes!
OK, better next time.
You choose!
You can do it!
You can get it done, it'll be worth it.
Keep at it, you'll get it finished.
Hang in there.
Be a stickler.

God loves a trier.
Good on you for persevering.
We all make mistakes. Don't give up!
Focus on this bit ...

Use encouraging signs
Thumbs up, smile, nod, touch on shoulder
Wink
Wave
Click click sound
Create choices in the classroom
Use warning systems that remind children they can make choices and take
responsibility for their behaviour.

Prioritise time: Get to know your class.

Use lots of games: Encourage friendship skills.
Playground Friends
Class swaps
Lunch-time clubs of shared interests
Buddy or mentoring systems
Peer mediation

Don't do these
Give superficial or indiscriminate praise. Temper with reality; be honest
with children, praise achievements, and don't tell them that everything they do
is perfect.

Leave children stewing about the error of their ways for any length of time.
Thinking about problems in a negative frame of mind produces fewer solutions.

Rehash the past.

Give in to sulking behaviour. This teaches children to get what they want by
being unhappy.

What children need to know
1. Give them practical methods
Appreciation audit: Try it at the end of the day by writing in Think Books, as a
class round, or in pairs. List five good things that have happened today – if
stuck start with routine things like: I got up, I had a cup of tea. Use The perfect
day worksheet on p. 63.

Secret stash: For a week, the class stashes anonymous notes into a box for one
child: 'What I really like about you is ...' (Check them before giving them to the
child, just in case.) Put yourself as the subject when you need cheering up.

Quick fix: Time in class – games, joke telling, physical activities, song, relaxation.

Art and other activities
Display: skills we can lend, things we can do to help other people, those we know, our special people at home or in school, those we don't know.

Two drawings: Draw a glass half full, and one half empty. Write the thoughts that make these so in bubbles around the glass. Discuss which they'd choose if they could have only one, and why. Do a round 'I like to think my glass is half full because …'.

'Always Look on the Bright Side of Life': Play the song, having approved the lyrics first, and ask children to paint a picture in two parts: on one side a symbol for their gloomy thoughts, and on the other a bright side version. Talk about why we need light and dark – some things in life will never be happy. Harbouring unrealistic optimism can make setbacks harder. What can we do if we get stuck on one side?

Seek, and ye shall find!: The children go in search of things around the school that they want a closer look at. They can make a booklet: 'The things I've seen'.

Beautiful people: Children photograph or sketch people enjoying being together. Identify the skills together.

Speak to Me of Love: Talk over the language of love, appreciation and gratitude. Agree on how we can express these feelings in the classroom. Provide some scripts on the wall in speech bubbles. Research symbols of love other than the heart and make a display of these.

2. Help them move toward feelings
Esteem: Esteem ourselves and each other with stars and stickers.

Have a Golden Child or Star of the Week: The class focus on and celebrate one particular child. Make sure everyone gets a turn.

Write in their Think Books: Something good that came out of something not so good today.

Charities: Set up or support a class charity, local or overseas.

Create a web link to another school overseas.

Body talk: Rhythmic activities such as song, dance and music can provide life-enhancing experiences.

Discuss what they can do to keep their bodies and brains happy or at peace.

Songs and music
'Walking in the Air' – Nightwish
'He Ain't Heavy, he's my Brother' – The Hollies
'Sun is Shining' – Bob Marley
'Little Fluffy Clouds' – The Orb
'Albatross' – Fleetwood Mac
'Hudson River Wind Meditations' – Lou Reed

Dance and film
When the class needs a boost, play a song and dance routine for 2–3 minutes. Sing and dance along.

3. Help them to direct

Give thanks: Set up a circle within another, the inner one having chairs facing out and the outer having chairs facing in. Pairs face each other. The person on the inside tells the other person one quality or gift they have noticed the listener displaying in school. The listener can say nothing except 'Thank you'. Encourage eye contact. Reverse roles.

4. Talk with them about feelings

Draw and Write: Use as a means to encourage them to talk with others about fear, worry and anxiety. Use the Were you happy or excited? worksheet on p. 64.

Word box: Collect related words.

Discuss: Compile a list of the products the children currently aspire to having. They debate these or create an alternative advert about why they don't want that product.

Bhutan in the Himalayas considers Gross National Happiness more important than Gross National Product. What can we do to increase our GNH?

Explore and discuss happiness traps – such as trying to buy happiness, find happiness from pleasure, be happy by resolving the past, be happy by overcoming weakness, forcing happiness.

The class could share their ideas of happiness and use the blue aid box or treasure chest of happiness for ideas.

Get children to do a sponsored no-television week. Give homework to write what they did instead and how this was.

Children's literature

What makes me Happy? – Catherine and Laurence Anholt
The Whales' Song – Dyan Sheldon and Gary Blythe
Wombat Goes Walkabout – Michael Morpurgo and Christian Birmingham
Pollyanna – Eleanor H. Porter

Bibliography

Baber, S. & N. Wetton (1994) *That's Like Me!*
Health Education Authority: London

Bombers, L.M. (2007) *Inside I'm Hurting*. Worth Publishing: London

Collins, M. & N. Wetton (2001) *Bullying Matters*.
Healthwise Helpline Limited: Liverpool

Corrie, C. (2003) *Becoming Emotionally Intelligent*.
Network Continuum: London

Damasio, A. (2004) *Looking for Spinoza*. Vintage: London

Erickson, M.H. (1980) *The Collected Papers of Milton H. Erickson on Hypnosis Vol. 4*. Irvington: New York

Gerhardt, S. (2004) *Why Love Matters*. Brunner-Routledge: East Sussex

Goleman, D. (2006) *Social intelligence*. Arrow Books Limited: London

Jenner, S. (2000) *The Parent/Child Game*. Bloomsbury: London

Lunzt, F. (2007) *Words that Work*. Hyperion: New York

Martin, P. (2005) *Making People Happy*. Fourth Estate: London

Mosley, J. (1993) *Turn Your School Round*. LDA: Cambridge

Mosley, J. & Z. Niwano (2007) *They're Driving me Mad!* LDA: Cambridge

Mosley, J. & H. Sonnet (2005) *Better Behaviour Through Golden Time*.
LDA: Cambridge

Mosley, J. & H. Sonnet (2006) *Using Rewards Wisely*. LDA: Cambridge

Oaklander, V. (1989) *Windows to Our Children*. Gestalt Journal Press: Pennsylvania

Robinson, K. (ed.) (1982) *The Arts in Schools*. Calouste Gulbenkian Foundation: London

Sunderland, M. (2001) *Using Story Telling as a Therapeutic Tool with Children*.
Speechmark: Milton Keynes

Sunderland, M. (2006) *The Science of Parenting*.
Dorling Kindersley Ltd: London

Wetton, N. & T. Williams (2000) *Health for Life Ages 4–7*.
Nelson Thornes: Cheltenham

Wetton, N. & T. Williams (2000) *Health for Life Ages 8–11*.
Nelson Thornes: Cheltenham

My helping hand

Everyone needs a helping hand sometimes.
Whom would you go to when you need help?

On each finger and the thumb, write
the name of someone you can talk to
if something is bothering you.

If you can't think what to write, ask
for help. At least three names must
be adults.

Draw one of the people you would ask to
help with your feelings.

I think this person is special because

....

....

I know I can trust them to help because

....

....

Keep this hand. Remember that there is
always someone to talk to if something is
bothering you.

Thinking about feelings

Draw and write your feelings in the boxes.

When I come to school I feel ...

In the classroom I feel ...

At playtime/lunchtime I feel ...

At home time I feel ...

Before I go to bed I feel ...

Draw and write about a part of the day you would like to be different.

Draw and write what you might need to think and/or say to make it different.

Angry time

We asked some children how you know when someone is angry.

Lots of children said you could see an angry body.

Draw a time when you were angry. Write any other feelings around you.

I am angry because ....

....

....

When I'm angry my body feels ....

....

....

and I want to ....

....

....

Write one hint for calming down when you are angry.

Were you angry?

Ask an adult you know well if you can interview them about their feelings when they were little. Ask them to remember a time when they felt annoyed or angry.

Invite them to draw a picture of this time on the back of this sheet (or be the artist for them) and get them to tell you about it.

Ask them to draw and write in the speech bubble and thought bubble.

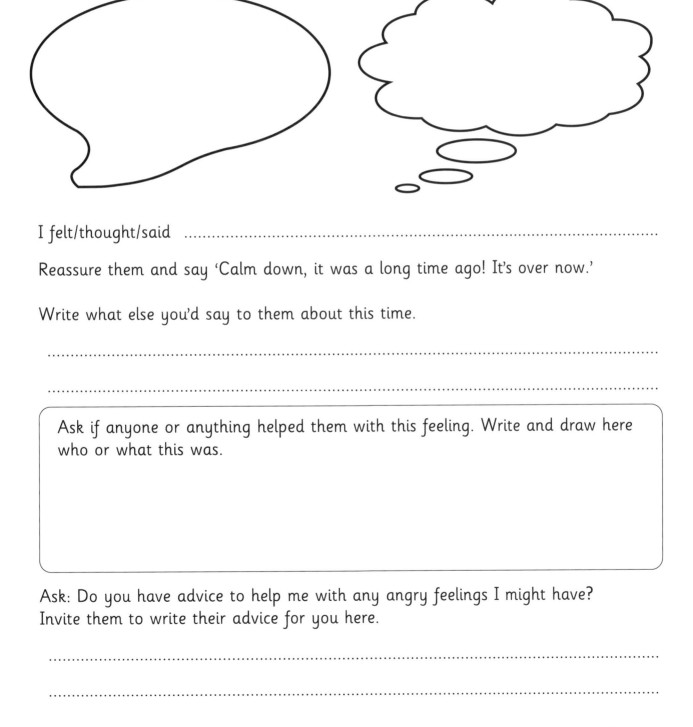

I felt/thought/said ....

Reassure them and say 'Calm down, it was a long time ago! It's over now.'

Write what else you'd say to them about this time.

....

....

Ask if anyone or anything helped them with this feeling. Write and draw here who or what this was.

Ask: Do you have advice to help me with any angry feelings I might have? Invite them to write their advice for you here.

....

....

Were you scared?

Ask an adult you know well if you can interview them about their feelings when they were little. Ask them to remember a time when they felt scared, worried or anxious.

Invite them to draw a picture of this time on the back of this sheet (or be the artist for them) and get them to tell you about it.

Ask them to draw and write in the speech bubble and thought bubble.

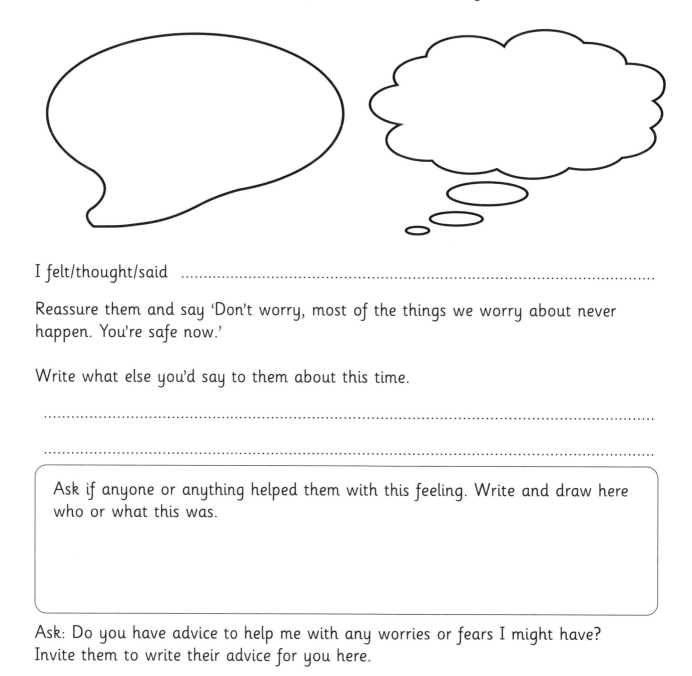

I felt/thought/said ....

Reassure them and say 'Don't worry, most of the things we worry about never happen. You're safe now.'

Write what else you'd say to them about this time.

....

....

Ask if anyone or anything helped them with this feeling. Write and draw here who or what this was.

Ask: Do you have advice to help me with any worries or fears I might have? Invite them to write their advice for you here.

....

....

All better

Sometimes we feel so full of hurt inside and a problem seems so big it is hard to imagine how to make it better.

1. Draw a picture of something you'd like to make better.

Now imagine it better.

2. Draw what that would look like.

Now think about how you can get from picture 1 to picture 2.
Write what you think you need to make it better.

I need

....

....

I will get help from

....

....

Now show this to an adult who can help you with a plan.

Were you sad and lonely?

Ask an adult you know well if you can interview them about their feelings when they were little. Ask them to remember a time when they felt sad or lonely.

Invite them to draw a picture of this time on the back of this sheet (or be the artist for them) and get them to tell you about it.

Ask them to draw and write in the speech bubble and thought bubble.

I felt/thought/said ....

Reassure them and say 'It's all right, I'm here with you now.'

Write what else you'd say to them about this time.

....

....

Ask if anyone or anything helped them with this feeling. Write and draw here who or what this was.

Ask: 'Do you have advice to help me with any sad feelings I might have?'
Invite them to write their advice for you here.

....

....

The perfect day

You are having the most perfect day. Think about where you are, what you are doing and how you are feeling.

Name some of the feelings you had during your perfect day.

Draw and write them here.

Explore the highlights of the day.

Write in each bubble …

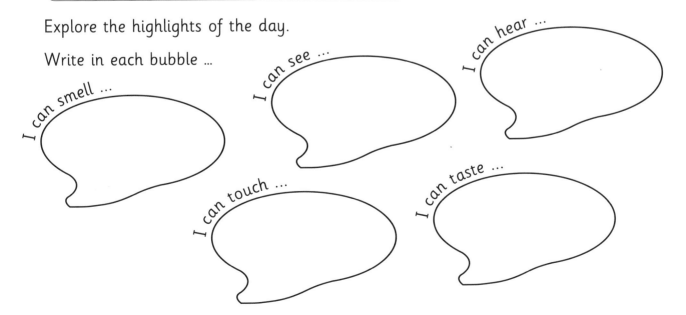

I can smell …

I can see …

I can hear …

I can touch …

I can taste …

Were you happy and excited?

Ask an adult you know well if you can interview them about their feelings when they were little. Ask them to remember a time when they felt happy or excited.

Invite them to draw a picture of this time on the back of this sheet (or be the artist for them) and get them to tell you about it.

Ask them to draw and write in the speech bubble and thought bubble.

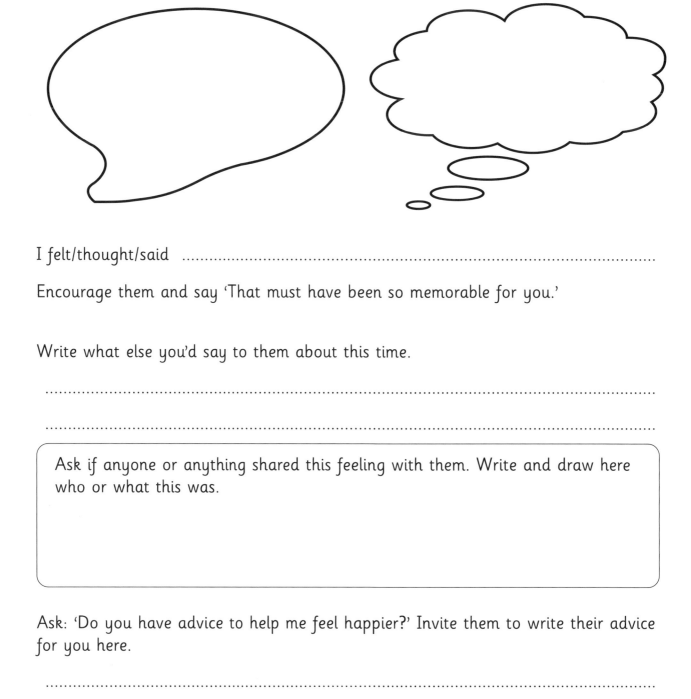

I felt/thought/said ....

Encourage them and say 'That must have been so memorable for you.'

Write what else you'd say to them about this time.

....

....

Ask if anyone or anything shared this feeling with them. Write and draw here who or what this was.

Ask: 'Do you have advice to help me feel happier?' Invite them to write their advice for you here.

....

....